Financial Crises

Lessons from Experiences

Bhubanesh Pant

ATLANTIC
PUBLISHERS & DISTRIBUTORS (P) LTD

Published by

ATLANTIC

PUBLISHERS & DISTRIBUTORS (P) LTD

7/22, Ansari Road, Darya Ganj, New Delhi-110002
Phones : +91-11-40775252, 40775214, 23273880, 23275880
Fax : +91-11-23285873
Web : www.atlanticbooks.com
E-mail : orders@atlanticbooks.com

Branch Office: Chennai
Phones : +91-44-48531784, 28291383
E-mail : chennai@atlanticbooks.com

Printed & bound in India by Atlantic Print Services

Preface

Financial crises are unavoidable. They appear to be an intrinsic feature of market-oriented credit and financial systems. As long as there are financial markets, there are bound to be boom and bust cycles. The last three decades have witnessed several financial crises in different parts of the globe. These crises became increasingly virulent, caused widespread disruption to both developing and advanced economies. In some instances, these crises were totally unexpected, and had affected countries which had enjoyed a strong economic performance up to that point in time.

In this respect, the financial debacle that followed the Mexican devaluation in December 1994 left many analysts and investors perplexed by its scale. It took place because of the unanticipated shocks and the poor policy responses to these shocks. Because of the crisis, the Mexican peso almost collapsed, and the government was close to default on its national debt. The level of foreign reserves plummeted significantly, and in the end the government needed a bailout to stay afloat financially.

Likewise, the crises that struck the miracle Asian economies during mid-1997 and the contagion they set in motion raised worries about the stability of the global financial system. In less than a year, East Asia was transformed from the world's fastest growing to the slowest growing region. The crisis exposed structural shortcomings and policy distortions in crisis-stricken economies, together with feebly planned financial liberalization and premature capital account opening.

Similarly, the Global Financial Crisis (GFC) began in July 2007 with the credit crunch, when a loss of confidence by US investors in the value of sub-prime mortgages caused a liquidity crisis. This, subsequently, resulted in the US Federal Reserve infusing a large amount of capital into financial markets. The collapse of Lehman Brothers on 15 September 2008 signalled the beginning of a new chapter in the GFC. Governments around the world struggled to rescue large financial institutions after the fallout from the housing and stock market collapse worsened.

While there may be country-specific factors leading to financial crises, there exist some common features. Given the crucial role of the financial sector, it is possible to take advantage of historical lessons and minimize the potential for future crises. And this is the crux of this book.

This book attempts to present a clear and straightforward account of the causes leading to the Mexican financial crisis of 1994, the East Asian financial crisis of 1997, and the GFC as well as draw lessons from their experiences. Some other financial crises have also been examined together with lessons derived from them. A few portions of Chapters 2 and 3 are based on my previous book entitled *Financial Crises, Recovery and Reforms* published in 2001, with updated information and analysis.

Finally, I hope that this book will be found useful by economists, bankers, policymakers, and others interested in this subject. Nonetheless, I am solely responsible for the gaps and omissions that may still exist.

Bhubanesh Pant

Contents

Abbreviations and Acronyms

ADB	Asian Development Bank
APEC	Asia-Pacific Economic Co-operation
ASEAN	Association of South East Asian Nations
BIBF	Bangkok International Banking Facility
BIS	Bank of International Settlements
CAR	Capital Adequacy Ratio
CPI	Consumer Price Index
ECB	European Central Bank
EDP	Excessive Deficit Procedure
EFSF	European Financial Stability Facility
EFSM	European Financial Stability Mechanism
EME	Emerging Market Economy
ESCAP	Economic and Social Commission for Asia and the Pacific
EU	European Union
FDI	Foreign Direct Investment
FDIC	Federal Deposit Insurance Corporation
FOBAPROA	Banking Fund for the Protection of Savings (Fondo Bancario de Protección al Ahorro)
FSI	Financial Soundness Indicator
GDP	Gross Domestic Product
GFC	Global Financial Crisis

GNP	Gross National Product
ILLR	International Lender of Last Resort
IMF	International Monetary Fund
LDC	Least Developed Country
NAFTA	North American Free Trade Agreement
NBFI	Non-Bank Financial Institution
NGO	Non-Governmental Organization
ODA	Overseas Development Assistance
OECD	Organization for Economic and Cooperation Development
PRI	Institutional Revolutionary Party (Partido Revolucionario Institucional)
PROCAPTE	Temporary Capitalization Program (Programa de Capitalizacion Temporal)
SAF	Structural Adjustment Facility
SAP	Structural Adjustment Program
SBA	Stand-by Arrangement
SDIF	Savings Deposit Insurance Fund
SME	Small and Medium Enterprise
SRF	Supplemental Reserve Facility
TARP	Troubled Asset Relief Program
UNCTAD	United Nations Conference on Trade and Development
WTO	World Trade Organization

Chapter 1

Introduction

1.1 Preamble

Financial crises are detrimental and contagious, demanding calls for rapid policy responses when they occur. As witnessed in the last few decades, crises can lead to deep and long-lasting recessions and can even trigger sharp current account reversals. A glance at a number of financial crises over the last few decades reveals a high degree of commonality: excessive exuberance, poor regulatory oversight, herd mentalities, unsustainable macroeconomic policies, excessive credit booms, large capital inflows, and balance sheet fragilities. A financial crisis is often linked with one or more of the following phenomena: significant changes in credit volume and asset prices; chronic disruptions in financial intermediation and the supply of external financing to different players in the economy; large scale balance sheet problems (of firms, households, financial intermediaries and sovereigns); and large scale government support (in the form of liquidity support and recapitalization). Thus, financial crises are typically multidimensional events and can be hard to characterize using a single indicator (Claessens and Kose, 2013).

However, not all crises are preceded by such events. Some crises can be contagious and swiftly spread to other countries with no apparent vulnerabilities.

Though literature has clarified some of the factors responsible for financial crises, it is still a challenge to clearly distinguish their deep-rooted causes. A number of theories have been formulated over the years with respect to the principal causes of the crises. While important factors—macroeconomic imbalances, internal or external shocks—are often cited, many questions remain on the precise causes of the crises. Financial crises sometimes appear to be driven by 'irrational' factors including sudden runs on banks, contagion and spillovers among financial markets, and other aspects related to financial turmoil.

Financial crises are often preceded by asset and credit booms that ultimately convert into busts. Many theories focusing on the sources of crises have acknowledged the significance of booms in asset and credit markets. However, understanding why asset price bubbles or credit booms are permitted to continue and eventually become unsustainable and convert into busts or crunches has been challenging. This requires finding an answer as to why neither financial market participants nor policymakers forecast the risks and try to slow down the expansion of credit and increase in asset prices.

Financial crises have domestic or external origins and can emanate from both private and public sectors. They come in different shapes and sizes, and evolve over time into different forms. Often, they need rapid and comprehensive policy responses, call for major changes in financial sector and fiscal policies, and can necessitate global coordination of policies.

Though many financial economists indicate the emergence of financial houses in thirteenth-century Italy as the origin of modern banking, one of the earliest crises on to date goes back to 33 A.D., when a confluence of actors—the sinking of some ships loaded with uninsured commodities, a slave revolt, fraud, defaults on foreign debt, liquidity-draining government policies, and a bout of domestic and international contagion—shut down a number of banking houses in Rome (Calomris, 1989). Tiberius Caesar overcame the crisis by providing government funds to safe bankers and certain debtors, forgiving some interest, and ending government policies that had temporarily drained liquidity. As a result, more financial institutions recovered.

This case notwithstanding, government safety nets were rare prior to the nineteenth century. Indeed, in many countries central banks were formally set up only in the twentieth century. Until then, market forces were relied on to tackle with bank insolvency, and depositors had no government safety net protecting their funds. Bank failures were quite widespread even in the United States, since many states had unit banks (banks with only one office). Their lack of diversification made these banks very susceptible to failure.

1.2 Types of Financial Crises

In terms of classification, there are broadly two types of financial crises that can be distinguished: those classified using strictly quantitative definitions and those dependent primarily on qualitative and judgmental analysis (Reinhart and Rogoff, 2009). While the first group mainly comprises currency and sudden stop crises, the second group contains debt and banking crises. Still, definitions are largely motivated by the theories attempting to explain crises.

While financial crises can take different shapes and forms, there have been a number of concrete definitions of many types of crises. For instance, a currency crisis consists of a speculative attack on the currency leading to a devaluation (or sharp depreciation), or compelling the authorities to defend the currency by spending huge amount of international reserves, or sharply raising interest rates, or enforcing capital controls. A sudden halt (or a capital account or balance of payments crisis) can be defined as a sizable (and often unexpected) decline in international capital inflows or a sharp reversal in aggregate capital flows to a country, likely taking place in combination with a sharp increase in its credit spreads.

Other crises are linked with adverse debt dynamics or banking system chaos. A foreign debt crisis occurs when a country cannot (or does not wish to) service its foreign debt. It can take the shape of a sovereign or private (or both) debt crisis. A domestic public debt crisis occurs when a country does not honor its domestic fiscal obligations in real terms, either by defaulting explicitly, or by inflating or otherwise debasing its currency, or by employing some other types of financial repression. In a systemic banking crisis, actual or potential bank runs and failures can cause banks to suspend the convertibility of their liabilities or force the government to intervene to stop this by extending liquidity and capital assistance on a massive scale.

Crises have adversely affected both developing countries and advanced countries. In the three decades before 2007, most crises occurred in developing countries including the Latin American crises in the late 1970s to early 1980s, the Mexican crisis in 1995, and the East Asian financial crisis in 1997. Developing countries being more prone to crises is not new (Reinhart and Rogoff, 2013). History reveals that many countries which are developed today witnessed financial crises when they were going through their own process of development, including Australia, Spain, the U.K. and the U.S. in the 1800s. Likewise, France defaulted on its external debt eight times during the period 1550-1800. Some advanced countries also experienced crises in recent decades such as the Nordic countries in the late 1980s and Japan in the 1990s. Likewise, the global financial crisis (GFC) originating in the U.S. in late 2007 and then extending to other developed countries exhibited that crises can impact all types of countries.

Some types of crises are more recurrent than others. Comparisons can be made for the post Bretton Woods period. While some types of crises have been recorded for longer periods, not all have; and currency crises were absent during the fixed exchange rate period. Of the total number of crises reported by Laeven and Valencia (2013), there are 147 banking crises, 217 currency crises, and 67 sovereign debt crises over the period 1970 to 2011, with many countries witnessing multiple crises of the same type.

There is some overlap between the various types of crises. Currency crises frequently tend to overlap with banking crises—the so-called twin crises (Kaminsky and Reinhart, 1999). In addition, sudden stop crises, not surprisingly, can overlap with currency and balance-of-payments crises, and sometimes sovereign crises. Of the 431 crises with banking (147), currency (217) and sovereign (67) crises reported by Laeven and Valencia (2013), they take 68 as twin crises, and 8 can be classified as triple crises. Relative differences in coincidences of these episodes also exist. A systemic banking crisis, for instance, often involves a currency crisis and a sovereign crisis sometimes overlaps with other crises.

Financial crises have become a global phenomenon. They seem to occur every now and then. At the same time, some countries have been adversely impacted more than others owing to differences in initial conditions (such as state of the economy, fiscal space, labor market, and institutional framework, among others) and exposure to direct and indirect effect of the crisis via credit and trade channels. In the past few decades, many crises have occurred. It started off with the Wall Street crash of October 1987. Two years later, Japan's stock market bubble collapsed; Europe's exchange rate mechanism had its tragedy in 1992-93; the bond market crashed in 1994; the Mexican crisis arose late in the same year; East Asia went into turbulence in 1997; and Russia's default and related shockwaves distressed the world in 1998. Problems in the financial sector were also encountered in Brazil in 1999 and Argentina in 2001. Likewise, the global financial crisis was triggered in 2007 followed by the Euro Debt Crisis in 2010.

1.3 Organization of the Study

The primary aim of this book is to present a critical review of some major financial crises and draw lessons from them. Chapter 2 discusses the financial crisis that struck Mexico in 1994. The situation in Mexico during the pre-crisis period is first summarized together with the events in 1994 that changed investor expectations about the Mexican economy and triggered the crisis. The causes and the consequences are then examined followed by the international bailout which drew much criticism. The policy actions undertaken to minimize the impact of the crisis are then underlined. Next, the effect of these policy actions are delineated after which the lessons that can be applied for minimizing the adverse impact of the crisis are highlighted.

In Chapter 3, the East Asian financial crisis that emanated in 1997 is discussed at length. The crisis began in Thailand in July 1997 and soon spread to East Asian countries primarily

Indonesia, Malaysia, Republic of Korea and Philippines. Because of excessive short-term debt across East Asia, capital inflows slowed or reversed. Banks ceded to high levels of nonperforming loans. And Asia's 'tiger' economies plunged into deep recessions. Hence, this chapter begins by examining the overall economic situation in the crisis-stricken countries prior to the crisis.[1] Weaknesses in the banking system just before the crisis such as low capital-adequacy ratios of banks, poor disclosure and transparency of bank operations and weak supervision are also described. This is followed by explaining how the crisis unfolded, especially by highlighting the case of Thailand where the crisis originated. Next, the major factors that led to the crisis are discussed together with the role of the IMF that provided financing packages to the crisis-affected countries. A list of lessons derived from the crisis are then analyzed.

A comprehensive review of the GFC is undertaken in Chapter 4. After elaborating on how the crisis emerged, the similarities of this crisis *vis-à-vis* some previous crises are also underlined along with the new features of this crisis including expansion of complex securities, financial integration, build-up of high degree of leverage of financial institutions and problems in the household sector. The impact of the GFC on the economies of developing countries coupled with the policies undertaken by these countries to minimize the adverse effects are also deliberated. Next, the impact of the GFC on the least-developed countries (LDCs) are elaborated, though the impact was less prominent initially since these countries are not as integrated into the global financial markets as some of the developed and developing countries.[2] The last section of Chapter 4 underlines the lessons drawn from the GFC.

Chapter 5 comprises a critical analysis of some of the previous financial crises as well as the lessons learnt from them. These include the Stock Market Crash of 1929 and the Great Depression, the international debt crisis in the 1980s, the Russian financial crisis of 1998, the Turkish financial crisis of 2001, the financial crisis of Argentina in 2001 and the European debt crisis of 2010.

The last chapter summarizes and concludes the study.

NOTES

1. In this study, the crisis-affected economies of East Asia specifically refer to Indonesia, Republic of Korea and Thailand and, to a lesser extent to Malaysia and the Philippines.
2. According to the UNCTAD (2018), 48 countries are designated as least developed: Afghanistan, Angola, Bangladesh, Benin, Bhutan, Burkina Faso, Burundi, Cambodia, Central African Republic, Chad, Comoros, Democratic Republic of the Congo, Djibouti, Eritrea, Ethiopia, Gambia, Guinea, Guinea-Bissau, Haiti, Kiribati, Lao People's Democratic Republic, Lesotho, Liberia, Madagascar, Malawi, Mali, Mauritania, Mozambique, Myanmar, Nepal, Niger, Rwanda, Sao Tome and Principe, Senegal, Sierra Leone, Solomon Islands, Somalia, South Sudan, Sudan, Timor-Leste, Togo, Tuvalu, Uganda, United Republic of Tanzania, Vanuatu, Yemen, and Zambia (UNCTAD, 2018).

Chapter 2

Financial Crisis in Mexico

2.1 Introduction

The Mexican financial crisis, also referred to as the 'Tequila Crisis', began after Mexico's devaluation of the peso in December 1994. It led to the worst banking crisis in Mexican history, the largest depreciation of the currency in a year, from about 5.3 pesos per dollar in December 1994 to over 10 pesos per dollar in November 1995, and the most severe recession in over a decade (with GDP plummeting to more than 6 percent in 1995) (Musacchio, 2012). The crisis spread to other Latin American countries (particularly Argentina and Brazil), and also converted into foreign exchange pressures on some Asian economies (such as Indonesia, Philippines and Thailand) as well as some advanced economies with poor economic fundamentals (Frankel, 1998).

The financial crisis that struck Mexico at the end of 1994 was a classic case of a country's determined adherence to a 'strong' currency. Its origins were deeply engrained in the history of a country that had witnessed election-year excesses and instability for decades. Nonetheless, for Mexico and for its major trading partners from Canada to Argentina, the crisis also had new and unique features that substantiated it being labelled "the first financial crisis of the twenty-first century."

2.2 Developments Prior to the Crisis

During the late 1980s and early 1990s, Mexico was regarded as a 'model economy.' During this period, a number of key economic reforms were implemented, with liberalization and privatization policies replacing the earlier model of state-led growth. Since these policies were executed with the support of the World Bank and the IMF, the Mexican case was deemed as a 'success story' by these organizations, which other Latin American countries were inspired to pursue. Owing to the positive impact of these neo-liberal economic policies, foreign investors began to invest on a massive scale in Mexico and over $90 billion poured into the country during 1990-93. Portfolio investments constituted almost two-thirds of these investments.

A host of external and internal factors were responsible for the massive upsurge in foreign investments in Mexico. The major external factor was low interest rates in the U.S. together with the recession there and in other countries as a result of which massive investment was directed into Mexico and elsewhere for higher profits. The Brady Plan of 1989 and Mexico's entry into the North American Free Trade Agreement (NAFTA) with the U.S. and Canada also improved Mexico's creditworthiness. The core internal factors that encouraged foreign investments were higher GDP growth rate at an average of 3.1 percent per year between 1988 and 1994, a low inflation rate which fell from almost 145 percent to just 6 percent, and extensive privatization of state-owned enterprises.[1]

Another factor for the upsurge in foreign investment was the return of the funds that had flowed out from Mexico to the U.S. during the Mexican debt crisis in the eighties. Anticipating an improvement in economic conditions in Mexico in the 1990s, the rich Mexicans brought back these funds.

A major portion of these inflows were short-term that aimed at making instant profits through financial speculation on stocks and other securities in Mexico's financial markets. Only a small portion of portfolio investments was used to build up new physical assets, such as factories or machinery. With the increased availability of foreign funds and growing dependence on them, Mexico faced a sharp drop in domestic savings, falling from 22 percent of the GDP in 1988 to 16 percent in 1994. Again, Mexico used these funds to finance its growing imports. Though exports from Mexico increased during this period, the import bill soared more quickly, leading to a high current account deficit of about $30 billion, equivalent to 8 percent of the country's GDP in 1994.

Between 1990 and 1994, portfolio investment inflows amounting to $71.2 billion were utilized by the Mexican authorities to finance 72 percent of its current account deficit. Reliance on portfolio inflows to finance the current account deficit resulted in higher financial costs in domestic currency. Because this was a boom period, department stores were packed with goods and consumer credit was provided liberally leading to the rise in the indebtedness of households and banks.

At the same time, Mexico was going through a host of political upheavals leading to the collapse of the peso and later of the economy. In January 1994, there was an armed rebellion by a peasant organization called the Zapatistas in the southern State of Chiapas. The Zapatistas were protesting against the NAFTA, Mexico's neo-liberal economic policies, and the lack of a true democracy. This resulted in political instability as the rebels fought with the police and armed forces for two weeks before both sides reached an agreement.

In March 1994, Luis Donaldo Colosio, a presidential candidate who represented Mexico's ruling party, the Institutional Revolutionary Party (PRI), was murdered at a public rally. And his assassination was just the beginning. A number of other political assassinations, kidnappings of high profile executives, an ongoing rise in U.S. interest rates, and violence in Chiapas continued to affect investors' perception of Mexico and led to a sizable outflow of capital from the country. These exoduses diminished the country's reserves of foreign exchange, a factor that also exacerbated investors' confidence in Mexico's exchange rate peg.

This was followed in September 1994 by the assassination of Party Secretary General Jose Francisco Ruiz Massier, another high-ranking PRI official. In December, there was repeated violence in Chiapas. Owing to these political uncertainties, foreign investors became cautious with their investments.

Though the occurrence of the crisis had little to do with economic fundamentals which had not seriously deteriorated, macroeconomic figures still disclosed that households were not raising their savings and that gross fixed investment was not going up, despite the rise in foreign borrowing. Domestic savings in Mexico went down from almost 18 percent of GDP in 1989 to 15 percent of GDP in 1994. This occurred while Mexicans raised their foreign borrowing from around zero percent of GDP in 1990 to more than 4 percent in 1993. That is, foreign borrowing was not utilized to raise investment. Aggregate demand rose as the government increased consumption. Since Mexicans were not increasing savings or investment, it was difficult to justify the expectation of future growth.

The country was also facing a credit boom, and inflation exceeded that of the United States, Mexico's main trading partner. Therefore, pressures on the peso peg increased during 1994. Again, goods imported into the country were growing cheaper and Mexican exports were becoming more expensive abroad, worsening the trade deficit. With a deteriorating trade deficit, Mexico had to borrow more to maintain the exchange rate. Investors were nervous as any large-scale reversal of capital flows could prompt a depreciation of the peso.

As these developments were taking place, Mexico's financial authorities were not able to undertake remedial measures, as Presidential elections were near, and any unpopular measure could have brought about the defeat of the then ruling party's candidate, Ernesto Zedillo.

Against this backdrop of political and economic instability, an election took place in Mexico in 1994. Ernesto Zedillo won the election by a large majority, promising to calm down the country. Still, Zedillo selected a new economic team, defying investor expectations that Pedro Aspe would continue as Minister of Finance. This amplified the speed of capital flight even more towards the end of November of 1994. On 20 December 1994, the Central Bank of Mexico took the major move to devalue the peso by 13 percent. The administration had discussed the plan with high profile entrepreneurs and union leaders to gradually depreciate the peso. It is not clear if information from this meeting was disclosed or not, but a panic spread quickly through financial markets on that day. In two days, investors took $5 billion out of Mexico. The magnitude of the capital outflow and the panic that began in financial markets compelled the government to float the peso.[2]

2.3 Responsible Factors

The deterioration in banks' balance sheets resulting from mounting loan losses was a vital factor leading up to the Mexican financial crisis. Deregulation of a financial system and rapid credit growth can have a very negative impact when banking institutions and their regulators do not have the resources and skills to maintain risk taking in check. A similar situation occurred in Mexico where the banks had been nationalized in 1982 and about 50 percent of their lending was provided to the government. When the banks were privatized in the early 1990s, they had no formal credit bureaus to monitor loans to households and small businesses to make certain that borrowers were not taking on excessive risk. Still, bank credit to private nonfinancial enterprises went up rapidly, from 10 percent of GDP in 1988 to more than 40 percent of GDP in 1994. This lending boom, which was greater than the screening and monitoring capabilities of the banks, took place due to both increased flows of savings into the banking sector and an increasing portion of bank lending directed to private firms.

The chief regulatory authority of banks in Mexico, the National Banking Commission, also did not have the capability to monitor banks' loan portfolios and management practices to stop inordinate risk taking. This lack of capabilities was exacerbated by the bank lending boom and by the massive expansion in lending by other financial institutions, such as credit unions, thrifts, and leasing companies. When Mexican banks and nonbank financial institutions increased their loan activities, they did indeed take on excessive risk, resulting in many bad loans. Non-performing loans soared from 4 percent of total loans in 1991 to 8 percent in mid-1994 (Frankel, 1998).

The rise in interest rates abroad was another primary factor responsible for the crisis. In February 1994, the U.S. Federal Reserve started to increase the interbank federal funds rate to curb incipient inflationary pressures from taking place. Though the policy was effective in keeping inflation in check in the U.S., the upward pressure it put on Mexican interest rates increased asymmetric information problems in the Mexican financial system. The rise in Mexican interest rates was also attributed to the steps undertaken by the central bank to safeguard the value of the peso.

Increases in uncertainty in Mexican financial markets and a stock market plunge triggered the full-blown financial crisis. Stock prices on the Bolsa fell nearly 20 percent between their peak in September 1994 and the middle of December 1994. The increase in uncertainty and fall in net worth raised asymmetric information problems by making it tough to differentiate good borrowers from bad and by increasing firms' incentives to take risky investments because they had less to lose if the investments failed.

There was a huge loss of international reserves arising from the intervention in the foreign exchange market by the Bank of Mexico to support the commitment to a pegged exchange rate. With the increasing uncertainty in the foreign exchange market, the government found it harder to finance its debt with peso-denominated bonds and so significantly increased its issues of dollar-denominated bonds. Though the Mexican Central Bank increased the interest rates sharply, the Mexican authorities were compelled to announce the devaluation of the peso on 20 December 1994.

The institutional structure of debt markets in Mexico then interacted with the peso devaluation to push the economy into a full-grown financial crisis. Devaluations are a highly nonlinear event since they result in an abrupt change in the exchange rate. With the peso halved in value by March 1995, there was a sharp increase in both actual inflation and expected inflation. Along with the wish of the Bank of Mexico and the Mexican Government to limit the peso depreciation, this rise in inflation instigated interest rates on debt denominated in pesos to rise to over 100 percent on an annual basis. The Mexican stock market tumbled sharply by another 30 percent in peso terms and more than 60 percent in dollar terms.

These asymmetric information impediments were critical for both domestic and foreign lenders. Foreign lenders, who had the difficulty in obtaining information about what was going on in the Mexican economy, quickly withdrew their funds. Foreign portfolio investment inflows to Mexico, which amounted to $20 billion a year in 1993 and early 1994, took an opposite path. By the beginning of the fourth quarter of 1994 outflows exceeded $10 billion at an annualized rate. The sharp deceleration in lending was also responsible for the collapse in economic activity, with real GDP growth falling from around 4-4.5 percent a year in the second half of 1994 to rates of around 10 percent in the second and third quarters of 1995 (Pant, 2001).

The economy weakened further as the breakdown in economic activity and the worsening in the cash flow and balance sheets of firms and households led to the aggravation of the banking crisis. A number of firms and households could not pay off their debts, leading to substantial loan losses for banks. Moreover, the depreciation of the Mexican currency had a direct adverse impact on the banks' balance sheets. The foreign currency-denominated liabilities of banks surged from 116.4 billion pesos at the end of December 1993 to 213.9 billion pesos at the end of December 1994, primarily owing to the fall in the value of the peso from 3.1 to the dollar to 5.3. This is depicted in Table 2.1.

Even more challenging for the Mexican banks was that a large portion of their foreign currency-denominated liabilities were very short term, so that the dramatic increase in the value of these liabilities generated liquidity problems as they had to be paid back quickly. Breakdown of the banking system would then have been unavoidable without any safety net of the government. But there was intervention by the Mexican Government, providing the funds to protect depositors and thus preventing a bank panic. However, as banks lost capital and wanted government support, they became less willing and able to lend.

Table 2.1: Foreign Currency Exposure of Mexican Banks

(Pesos, in billions)

	Dec-93	Dec-94	Mar-95	Jun-95	Sep-95	Dec-95
Aggregate Banking System						
Foreign Currency Denominated Assets						
Tesobonos	0.4	3.6	1.4	0.8	0.4	0.0
Securities	1.5	6.3	6.4	9.1	11.5	22.5
Loans	54.0	99.2	130.5	126.7	124.4	146.3
Assets of Branches & Agencies	67.3	116.8	132.7	123.7	121.9	142.4
Total	123.2	225.9	271.0	260.3	258.2	311.2
Foreign Currency Denominated Liabilities						
In Mexico	49.1	97.1	136.2	121.2	119.9	154.9
In Branches & Agencies	67.3	116.8	132.7	123.7	121.9	142.4
Total	116.4	213.9	268.9	244.9	241.8	297.3
Exposure						
Foreign Assets Minus Foreign Liabilities	6.8	12.0	2.1	15.4	16.4	13.9
Foreign Assets/Total Assets	15.6%	28.6%	29.7%	27.7%	27.3%	29.9%
Foreign Liabilities/Total Liabilities	14.7%	27.0%	29.5%	26.0%	25.6%	28.6%
Exchange Rate	3.1059	5.325	6.8175	6.3092	6.4195	7.6425

Source: Mishkin (1996).

2.4 Devaluation and Financial Turmoil

While Mexico's devaluation came as a shock to many, there were indications that a crisis might have been developing. By early 1994, the peso seemed to be somewhat over-valued; the question was whether the overvaluation could be rectified without exploding into a financial crisis. For many months, the government attempted to avoid a decisive action by maintaining the exchange rate peg while leaving other elements of the policy largely untouched. Ultimately, the government was forced to devalue.

Though many analysts had predicted that sooner or later there would be a devaluation of the peso, no one had expected the financial crisis which ensued. The events which followed the devaluation demonstrate that there was a serious miscalculation of the potential response of financial markets to the peso devaluation. The instant reaction of the investors that had held their funds in the stock market or in other instruments was to pull out their funds rapidly. And toward the second week of January 1995, Mexico was on the brink of default and the financial markets of Latin America started to be adversely impacted.

The devaluation and its mishandling produced massive losses to the investors. Foreigners who had invested in the Mexican stock markets, Cetes, Tesobonos and Brady bonds, lost more than US$ 30 billion (Lustig, 1995).[3] They resented the government's reiterated refusal that a devaluation would take place, the fact that it did not realign the exchange rate when it was 'natural' or, otherwise, increase domestic interest rates to defend the prevailing exchange rate policy. Investors were also distressed by the lack of competence with which the government managed the devaluation itself. A coherent macroeconomic plan at the time of the devaluation was lacking.

Some portfolio investors viewed the devaluation as unnecessary and counterproductive. These investors contend that the exchange rate was not overvalued and that the financial crisis was basically endogenous, that is, caused by the change in expectations precipitated by the devaluation and the government's poor handling of it. The IMF, the World Bank and the U.S. Treasury were also blamed for the crisis since, in different stages, they had been advising the Mexican Government to devalue. Some had gone to the limit of prescribing as a solution to employ all the resources available to the Mexican Government to buy pesos and return to the pre-December parity of 3.46 peso to the dollar (Malpass, 1995). Once this level was attained, Mexico should have set up a currency board and fix the exchange rate at that rate.

Another group of investors felt disappointed since the government had the option of a 'soft landing' and did not undertake it. According to this view, increasing domestic interest rates would have, on the one hand, lowered the current account deficit owing to its recessionary impacts, and, on the other, attracted more capital as a response to the rise in yields. For this group it was rational to lower economic growth to defend the parity of the peso since, in due course, structural reform and NAFTA would raise the growth rate in productivity adequately to make the nominal exchange rate policy congruent with the required real 'equilibrium' exchange rate. Though in the short-run the 'soft-landing' option implied a recession, in the medium term the outcome would be price stability and growth.

Part of the investors' disappointment emanated from the perception, which turned out to be correct, that the fiscal and monetary policies executed by the government in 1994 were not consistent with the exchange rate rule. On the fiscal side, the public sector borrowing requirement had, in fact, gone up by more than two percentage points due to the development banks' net lending. Monetary policy ran counter to the exchange rate rule because rather than maintaining domestic interest rates high in the background of rising interest rates in the U.S., they were permitted to fall at a time when reserves were dwindling. All in all, investors' reactions, justified or not, resulted in the peso to sliding much beyond the prediction.

Another crucial contributing factor to the debacle of the peso was the replacement of almost all the total short-term government debt from Cetes to Tesobonos as it increased the risk of default significantly. Immediately after the devaluation, portfolio investors began to express their concern that the Mexican Government would be compelled to declare the inconvertibility of the peso. This concern rose when investors saw that payments coming due in 1995 (estimated at about US$ 50 billion assuming that most of the short-term debt would not be rolled-over) exceeded the estimated resources available: international reserves in the Bank of Mexico were about US$ 6 billion and the first international rescue package was equal to US$ 18 billion (Lustig, 1995). The rescue package together with the reserves would just encompass half of Mexico's financial obligations for 1995.

To soothe the markets and halt the financial meltdown, it was evident that the rescue package had to be large enough to set aside fears of a default to rest. Otherwise, the panic selling and its spread to other markets would not be stopped. To stop the panic it was vital to find a lender of last resort. With this in mind, the U.S. administration prescribed a package of loan guarantees of US$ 40 billion in the middle of January 1995. Unfortunately, the package encountered great hurdles in the Congress. When it was clear that it might not be approved, the U.S. administration recommended an alternative plan and the IMF raised its financial support sharply. At the end of January 1995, the U.S. Government declared that there was a financial package ready of approximately US$ 50 billion.

The announcement of the package ended the panic selling but did not reinstate long-term confidence. This was partly attributed to the fact that the rescue package did not make all the funds instantly available. However, to a large degree, the lack of confidence originated in the uncertainty surrounding the path of the economic and political atmosphere in Mexico. Strangely, IMF endorsement of the economic plan did not reinstate the confidence of the markets either. There were many questions over whether the targets of the economic program announced at the beginning of January were realistic. It was clear that they were not; especially, the exchange rate presumed in the plan of 4.5 pesos to the dollar was beyond reach.

In early 1995, the primary challenge for the Mexican Government was the restoration of its credibility. To achieve this, it was crucial to implement a program with realistic goals, ensure that short-term real interest rates would be positive, stipulate clear monetary, fiscal and exchange rate policies and provide, in a regular and transparent way, the information required to monitor the program. The markets started to react positively towards the end of March more as a result of economic outcomes than intentions. Especially, the markets appeared to appreciate the trade surplus in January and February 1995, the higher domestic interest rates, and the significant reduction in outstanding Tesobonos. The fact that the U.S. interest rates would not continue to go up also helped to bolster the turnaround.

2.5 Role of Nonperforming Loans

There was a steady rise in the share of nonperforming loans in the course of the crisis. The ratio of nonperforming to total loans in the balance sheet of commercial banks rose from almost 9 percent at the end of 1994 to 16 percent in 1995 and further to 21 percent in 1996 as depicted in Table 2.2. In 1997, this ratio went up further to almost 30 percent, primarily ascribed to a change in banking regulation that instructed banks to classify the principal in addition to the unpaid interest as non-performing. However, these figures exclude the banks' loans that were already transferred to the central bank in exchange for government bonds under FOBAPROA and the UDIs programs.[4, 5]

Table 2.2: Ratio of Nonperforming Loans to Total Loans

	1995	1996	1997
Average	16.4	21.4	29.8
Firms	18.5	21.9	27.0
Households	12.0	18.3	38.0
Consumption	25.2	34.2	28.3
Credit Cards	19.5	23.0	19.1
Durable Consumer Goods	44.2	67.1	55.6
Housing	7.9	12.2	42.0
Non-bank Intermediaries	10.7	28.9	49.4

Source: Krueger and Tornell (1999).

Table 2.2 illustrates the distribution of bad loans across a spectrum of various users. In December of 1997, the most impacted sector was 'durable consumption goods' with a nonperforming ratio of about 55 percent. The corresponding ratios for housing loans and for firms stood at 42 percent and

27 percent, respectively. However, these figures only include the non-intervened banks and do not include loans transferred to the government under FOBAPROA and the UDIs programs.

The share of nonperforming loans mentioned above did not imply that the remaining loans in the balance sheets of the non-intervened banks were by default performing loans. This is because a part of these loans were nonperforming loans that were not officially acknowledged by the banks as such. These included the so-called 'evergreen accounts', where the bank in question lent the debtor the principal and interest that the debtor was supposed to have repaid.[6]

What is surprising during 1996 and 1997 is that the high GDP growth did not result in a rise in bank lending and to a reduction in the share of nonperforming loans. In theory, high GDP growth would lead to a rise in firms' profits and household incomes. Consequently, debtors would have been able to service their debts, and banks would have been able to increase credit. However, a few reasons can be cited as to why this did not take place in Mexico.

In the first place, there was an absence of transparent and effective bankruptcy procedures in the country, making it almost impossible to take possession of a debtor's assets in case it failed to service its debt. This problem was only worsened by the financial crisis. Thus, real domestic lending rates were much higher than interest rates at which large tradable firms could procure financing in world markets. As a result, Mexican banks lost 'good customers' and were left with firms that were not accessible to global capital markets either because they were small or because their earnings were not in dollars. The worsening in the pool of borrowers and the related reduction in the expected rate of return led to an unwillingness of banks to provide higher interest rates in order to attract more deposits.

Another factor for the increase in the share of bad loans despite the high GDP growth was that while the banks lowered their net lending they were at the same time saddled with the above discussed evergreen accounts. As these accounts were *de facto* nonperforming loans, the accrued interest must have been capitalized every period. As a result, evergreen accounts grew exponentially, lowering the capacity of banks to provide new loans to fresh projects. Since each period a portion of the evergreen debtors went bankrupt, and since net total lending was declining, the outcome was a rise in the share of reported nonperforming loans.

A third reason for the upsurge in the share of bad loans was the existence of severe moral hazard problems in the banking system. On the one hand, the absence of transparent and effective bankruptcy procedures coupled with the fact that the crisis left many borrowers insolvent created the incentives for some debtors with the capacity to service their debts not to do so, since nonpayment would be hardly penalized. On the other hand, the presence of evergreen accounts left a number of banks with negative effective capital. This meant that their capital became smaller than the sum of the recognized and unrecognized nonperforming loans. When banks possess negative effective capital, managers have incentives to execute risky projects with a negative net expected value.

2.6 Impact of the Crisis

A visible recession and a banking crisis followed the devaluation. As investors moved out of the country, interest rates in Mexico surged quickly, forcing many consumers and businesses who had borrowed funds from commercial banks or from foreigners to default on their loans.

The fragility of the banking system became obvious as defaults rose rapidly in 1995. The percentage of nonperforming loans as a percentage of total loans of Mexican commercial banks increased sharply as discussed in Section 2.5. Consequently, the Bank of Mexico and the National Banking Commission initiated a major bailout and cleaning of the system. The bailout can be described in terms of three major programs. First, the government created a trust fund named PROCAPTE (funded from the FOBAPROA deposit insurance fund and with funds from the Central Bank).[7] This fund lent the banks capital sufficient to maintain a 9 percent capital ratio in exchange for five-year subordinated debentures from the bank. In the case of non-payment, the debentures were convertible to ordinary stock that the government could sell (Haber, 2005). Banks were not permitted to pay dividends or issue further debt until they repaid these funds. Second, the government introduced a special dollar credit window to help banks pay for their dollar-denominated debt.

Finally, the government helped banks in cleaning their balance sheets of nonperforming loans utilizing the funds from FOBAPROA. It basically exchanged bonds for non-performing loans. On paper, the banks were still responsible for collecting interest and principal repayments for those loans, but in practice this method became a way to write off loans and hand them on to the government. When banks plunged into severe financial distress, the National Banking Commission intervened, cleaning up their balance sheets using FOBAPROA funds, and then selling the banks to new investors, normally foreign banks. Of the 27 commercial banks that operated in Mexico in 1995, the National Banking Commission had intervened in 7 commercial banks by 1996.

2.7 The Bailout

In 1995, Mexico faced the worst recession in its history and capital flight persisted, both destabilizing financial markets and leading to further depreciation of the peso. A number of mutual and pension funds from the United States and other countries that had some of their capital locked in Mexico witnessed its value plunge even further that year. Moreover, as the economy continued to subside, there was contagion to other developing economies. Robert Rubin, the then Treasury Secretary of the United States, warned in 1995 that a further collapse of the peso and of the Mexican economy could have adverse impact on economies around the world. That year President Bill Clinton and a Treasury Department team including Rubin and Undersecretary Lawrence Summers arranged for a large scale standby loan for Mexico. The purpose was to open a line of credit to Mexico large enough to stop any speculative attack that could further destabilize the peso and the Mexican economy. The credit line was for $50 billion, of which the U.S. Treasury provided $20 billion; the remainder came from the IMF ($18 billion), the BIS ($10 billion), and private sector banks (about $3 billion). The Mexican Government used only approximately $13 billion from the U.S. Treasury and repaid the money rather quickly. The loan did assist in stabilizing the Mexican economy. Overall, total disbursements amounted to only $26.7 billion.

This type of international bailout, nevertheless, generated some criticisms. Critics viewed that the bailout produced moral hazard and that after the Mexican experience other countries could expect to receive a similar bailout package, particularly from the IMF. The bailout, the critics argued, undermined incentive to maintain macro discipline and, especially, discipline in the management of foreign debt, for instance, in the case of Argentina in 2001 (Vasquez, 2002).

Ultimately, the Mexican crisis brought about a few minor changes in the international financial architecture. Yet those changes were insignificant and could not avoid the Asian financial crisis of 1997-98 as well as the Argentine default of 2001. In the aftermath of the Mexican crisis and the international bailout, the G-7 released a communiqué at the Halifax Summit in the summer of 1995 that highlighted the need of emergency funding facilities at the IMF that had upfront access and quicker procedures. This resulted in the creation of the supplemental reserve facility at the IMF in 1997. Further, the communiqué also proposed the need to double the resources available through the backup credit line that the G-10 countries provided to the IMF and an IMF quota review to raise the IMF's lending capacity (Musacchio, 2012).

2.8 Steps Undertaken

The challenge for economic policy was not only to reduce the current account deficit but also to formulate and execute measures to avert the collapse of the financial and productive sectors. Hence, along with fiscal and monetary adjustments, the adoption of a floating exchange rate, and advances in structural reform and market liberalization, the Mexican

Government negotiated an emergency financial package with the U.S. Government, the IMF, the World Bank, and the Inter-American Development Bank in order to avoid suspending payments on the country's external obligations. This financial package was also essential in order to prevent the crisis from spreading over to other countries.

Preventive steps were also taken on the domestic financial market in order to avoid contagion through a rescue package to assist banks and borrowers alike, and stop the widespread collapse of financial institutions. The package comprised the following: (a) provision of liquidity in foreign exchange by the central bank to commercial banks to stop them from becoming delinquent on their foreign obligations; (b) activation of a program to provide temporary capital to banks and a subsequent program to raise the incentives for distressed banks; (c) legal reforms to allow more foreign equity participation in banks; and (d) programs to support selected categories of bank debtors.

The undergoing paragraphs briefly discuss the salient features of the major economic policies included in the revised program for 1995.

Monetary policy was targeted at checking inflationary pressures and reducing exchange rate volatility. This policy, subsequently, promoted: (a) the roll-over of foreign liabilities; (b) the resumption of long-term capital flows towards Mexico, mainly direct foreign investment and export credits from Exim banks; (c) increases in international reserves; and (d) progressive declines in interest rates, as inflation expectations improved.

With respect to fiscal policy, a rise in the primary surplus was needed to help attain a decline in interest rates and inflation, and lower the economy's reliance on foreign resources. Prices of public goods and services soared in 1995. For example, there was a rise in the price of gasoline and diesel: an initial 35 percent plus 0.8 percent per month, for a 48.5 percent total annual increase. The price of railway, airport and highway services rose 2.5 percent per month. Moreover, beginning 1 April 1995, the general VAT increased from 10 to 15 percent, except at border locations.

Current expenditures were slashed by 9.7 percent in real terms. The major drop was in wages and salaries, which went down by 9 percent in real terms *vis-à-vis* those paid in 1994. New investment projects were deferred and non-priority projects were implemented at a slower pace.

The aim of exchange rate policy was to reduce fluctuations in the foreign exchange market. To achieve this, certain measures were executed: (a) the floating exchange rate regime adopted at the outset of the crisis was maintained; (b) exchange rate stability was to be attained basically by containing the growth of net domestic credit; and (c) resources could be used by the Bank of Mexico from the Exchange Stabilization Fund to restrain volatility.

Further, operations in futures, forwards, and options markets were allowed in order to (a) facilitate decision-making, especially in the foreign trade sector; (b) reduce volatility in the exchange rate and interest rates; (c) lower pressures on the spot market; (d) provide economic agents access to these markets through authorized Mexican banks, the Mexican Stock Exchange and the Chicago Mercantile Exchange; (e) use the resources in the Exchange Stabilization Fund, received from the U.S. Treasury and other institutions, to substitute medium-term public debt for short-term debt; and (f) ensure that the banking system fulfilled its commitments overseas through the use of these resources.

The following measures were taken to protect lower-income and rural workers: (a) social security medical coverage was temporarily prolonged for laid-off workers, from 2 to 6 months; (b) the federal and state governments implemented a temporary rural jobs program to support workers in that sector; and (c) cash subsidy payments for the production of basic agricultural products were raised together with consumption subsidies for tortilla, bread and milk.

2.9 Impact of the Measures

After the devaluation in December 1994, the trade balance shifted from a deficit to a surplus in just two months' time. In the third month after the devaluation, the interest rate started to go down, the exchange rate fluctuation was lowered, and the current account deficit began to improve.

In the eighth month after the devaluation, Mexico was back in the capital markets again. Since April 1995, Mexican banks gradually rolled over their foreign liabilities and acquired new credits overseas. The public sector regained access to international capital markets in May 1995, only five months following the crisis.

However, the recovery came only after a number of distressing steps. The measures implemented were very costly. Yet, the results were encouraging. Although GDP plummeted by 6.2 percent in 1995, it recuperated, with growth of 5.2 percent in 1996 and 7 percent in 1997. Other favorable economic indicators were the unemployment rate, which went down from 7.6 percent in August 1995 to 3.5 percent in February 1998 and inflation, which dropped drastically from 52 percent in 1995 to 15.7 percent in 1997.

The floating exchange rate also performed satisfactorily. The Bank of Mexico's goal was price stability and for attaining that, it maintained strict monetary discipline supported by sound fiscal policy. The current account deficit, which averaged 6.7 percent of GDP in 1992-94, was lowered to an average of 1 percent of GDP in 1995-97. International reserves soared by more than $25 billion from January 1995 to January 1998. Total net public sector debt dropped from 39 percent of GDP in 1995 to 27 percent of GDP in 1997. The rate of domestic saving rose significantly, from 15 percent of GDP in 1994 to about 25 percent in 1997.

2.10 Lessons Drawn

A few lessons can be drawn from Mexico's experience with the crisis. One, openness to international financial markets inflicts an obligation of certain discipline on economic policy (Camdessus, 1995). Vigilance and discipline provide the most appropriate prevention and defense against financial market setbacks. Mexico's crisis showed clearly the costs that can come about when a country lowers its guard and permits markets to exercise their discipline instead.

Two, sizable current account deficits are risky, particularly when they are being utilized to support domestic consumption and are being financed by short-term capital inflows. They are risky since they are not likely to be sustainable. This was applicable even when, as in Mexico's case, the fiscal position was strong, and the current account deficit largely indicated weak private sector saving. With the benefit of hindsight, Mexico's fiscal position should have been even stronger to curb the country's reliance on easily reversible capital inflows.

Hence, unsustainable current account deficits should be circumvented, especially for longer periods (more than one or two years) (Griffith-Jones, 1997). It is not easy to establish in advance what levels of current account deficit are sustainable. However, it is generally agreed that for countries growing at 5 percent per annum or less, the current account deficit should not be greater than 3-4 percent of GDP. For countries with faster growth, where a large proportion of the current account deficit is invested rather than consumed, and where the deficit is funded primarily by long-term capital flows, the maximum advisable current account deficit could be somewhat, but not very much, higher.[8]

Three, Mexico's devaluation showed not only that it was tough to adjust a pegged exchange rate even when such a change was called for, but also that sound and credible accompanying macroeconomic measures were necessary to provide a firm basis for market expectations and to make the new exchange rate sustainable.

Four, Mexico's crisis showed the costs of failure to publish and disseminate regularly accurate information pertaining to core economic indicators. The crisis emerged in the way it did partly because the scale of the problem only became obvious at the time of the devaluation and took the financial markets by surprise. If data relating to international reserves and other key variables had been published more regularly and with a shorter time lag, the efficiency of market discipline and the chances of a smoother adjustment would undoubtedly have been enhanced.

Five, clear lessons pertaining to the management of the stock of public debt can also be drawn from the Mexican financial crisis. Policymakers should avoid assuming the foreign exchange risk in short-term government debt (as the Mexican authorities did on a large scale by issuing large amounts of Tesobonos). Furthermore, it is appropriate to change the structure of government debt towards more long-term paper, even if this denotes somewhat higher costs in interest payments. Specifically, large scale purchases by foreigners of short-term government debt need to be avoided. Because of the focus of Tesobonos' maturities in the short end of the spectrum, the Mexican situation got out of control in January 1995.

Six, another lesson from the crisis is that in very open economies, it is necessary to have far higher foreign exchange reserves than in the past owing to the volatility of capital flows. Large decline in foreign exchange demand a quick policy response and should never be dismissed as a temporary problem.

Seven, there were two specific important areas of regulation, whose need was underscored by the Mexican experience. First, there is a need to take account of exchange rate risks properly, and second, the fact that exchange rate risk becomes credit risk when there is a large devaluation and may result in sharp increases in bad loans. If a bank borrows in foreign exchange, even if it lends in foreign exchange, there is an indirect but crucial exchange rate risk, as in the situation of a large devaluation when the borrower may become bankrupt and hence unable to pay. The Mexican and other regulators did not fully consider this risk.

Eight, simply cleaning the balance sheets of banks and privatizing them is not adequate to ensure good banking practices. It is also vital to set up an effective regulatory framework and devise adequate bankruptcy procedures to ensure that creditors can take possession of the collateral in case of non-performance.

Nine, when a strong regulatory framework does not exist, financial deregulation could result in a lending boom, subsequently producing vulnerabilities in the banking system.

If domestic credit increases too quickly, the quality of the banks' portfolios worsens. Hence, even a trivial negative shock can push many loans into nonperforming status, and result in banking crises. Further, the presence of nonperforming loans is an impediment for the banking system to adequately perform its functions.

Ten, the composition of capital inflows is very crucial. Short-term flows are quite sensitive to short-term changes in interest rates and other political and macroeconomic variables. Long-term direct investment funds, on the other hand, are less volatile and do not react to short-term speculative factors. Maintaining short-term capital under control while fostering long-term investment is a move in the right direction.

Appendix 2.1: Mexico's Financial Crisis: Chronology of Important Events

1994	Events
1 Jan.	NAFTA becomes effective; Chiapas rebels (Zapatista Army of National Liberation) capture six towns.
4 Feb.	U.S. Federal Reserve increases federal funds rate by 25 basis points, having left the rate unchanged at 2 percent since September 1992.
22 Mar.	U.S. Federal Reserve raises rates by another 25 basis points.
23 Mar.	Mexican presidential candidate Luis Donaldo Colosio is assassinated.
18 Apr.	U.S. Federal Reserve increases rates by another 25 basis points. Zapatista Army of National Liberation breaks peace talks.
17 May	U.S. Federal Reserve raise rates by 50 basis points.
16 Aug.	U.S. Federal Reserve increase rates by another 50 basis points.
21 Aug.	Victory for PRI candidate Ernesto Zedillo in the Mexican presidential election.
15 Nov.	U.S. Federal Reserve raises rates by 75 basis points.
18 Nov.	US$ 1.6 billion flows out of Mexico (US$ 3 billion during the entire month).
30 Nov.	New cabinet is formed; stock market starts to decline.
1 Dec.	New Mexican government under Zedillo takes office.
15 Dec.	*Wall Street Journal* publishes interview with the new Finance Minister Jaime Serra Puche; US$ 855 billion goes out of Mexico on that day.
19 Dec.	Further violence in Chaipas.
20-21 Dec.	Bank of Mexico discloses sensitive information to business and labor leaders; $4.6 billion goes out of Mexico in two days.

22 Dec.	Bank of Mexico declares 15 percent shift in the intervention limits for the peso, an effective devaluation of the currency.
1995	
11 Jan.	President Clinton announces support for Mexico.
15 Jan.	Direct talks between Mexican government and Zapatista rebels begin.
26 Jan.	Mexico signs letter of intent accepting IMF conditionality in return for a loan of US$ 7.8 billion.
31 Jan.	The U.S. announces a US$ 50 billion loan package for Mexico, comprising of US$ 20 billion from the U.S., US$ 18 billion from the IMF (including the US$ 7.8 billion noted above), US$ 10 billion from the BIS, and US$ 3 billion from private commercial banks.
21 Feb.	Mexico and the U.S. sign loan agreement; military attacks against the Zapatista Army of National Liberation resume.
3 Mar.	Mexican authorities take control of a private bank (Banpais) as crisis grips the domestic financial system.
9 Mar.	Mexican government comes out with a new reform and stabilization plan.

Source: Musacchio (2012).

NOTES

1. The domestic factors that attracted foreign investment are elaborated in *The Economist*, 28 October 1995.
2. The important events of the financial crisis in Mexico are summarized in Appendix 2.1.
3. Cetes, which stands for *Certificado de la Tesorería de la Federación*, refer to the Mexican Federal Treasury Certificates and are investment instruments provided by the Federal Government via the Ministry of Finance and Public Credit and the Bank of Mexico. Tesobonos indicate bonds in which the coupon and/or redemption value are linked to the movement in an exchange rate.

4. FOBAPROA or Banking Fund for the Protection of Savings referred to the contingencies fund developed in 1990 by the Mexican Government and the then dominant political party PRI to attempt to resolve liquidity problems of the banking system. FOBAPROA was applied in 1995 during the crisis to safeguard all Mexican banks from going bankrupt (OECD, 1997).
5. It was in 1995 that Mexico launched a credit system based on a price-level-adjusting unit of account called the Unidad de Inversión (UDI). The Bank of Mexico maintains an UDI Index, which fixes the peso value of an UDI on any given day. Loans denominated in UDIs uphold their purchasing power and offer a real rate of return in the local currency.
6. Though these transfers were accounted as 'loans', they were *de facto* capitalized nonperforming loans (Krueger and Tornell, 1999).
7. PROCAPTE was a temporary capitalization fund set up in March 1995 to inject capital in the banking system in the form of mandatory convertible subordinated debentures.
8. According to Lee (1998), however, though current account sustainability cannot be defined technically, under most cases the current account deficit should rarely be greater than 3 percent of GDP in the long run.

Chapter 3

Financial Crisis in East Asia

3.1 Introduction

The East Asian countries were for years admired as very successful EMEs, owing to their rapid growth and the rise in the living standards of their people. With their generally prudent fiscal policies and high rates of private saving, they were viewed as paragons for many other countries. No one could have envisaged that these countries could become involved in one of the worst financial crises of the postwar period.

The East Asian financial crisis took prominence in 1997 because of its totally unforeseen nature and the magnitude of destruction it wrought. The crisis was a series of currency devaluations and other events that started in July 1997 and extended through many Asian markets. The currency markets first failed in Thailand owing to the government's decision to no longer peg the domestic currency to the U.S. dollar. Currency declines spread rapidly throughout East Asia, subsequently leading to stock market declines, reduced import revenues and government upheaval, among others.

The crisis had grave repercussions for the 'miracle' economies of East Asia, for developing countries in general and for the financial markets globally. It generated a heated debate on vital issues on economics, finance and economic policy-making in general.

3.2 Developments Prior to the Crisis

The sustained rapid growth of most of the crisis-stricken economies, averaging about 8 percent per year prior to the onset of the crisis, was attributed to their high rates of saving and investment. Their records in saving and investment were reinforced by sound macro-economic policies that resulted in budget surpluses with low inflation and stable exchange rates for favorable business environment. Moreover, more attention was given to education for ensuring future competitiveness. While issues such as the environmental degradation were also underscored, there was no warning on the advent of the crisis. It was assumed that the relatively high growth rates would continue, *albeit* at a reduced rate, as income levels in these economies touched advanced economy levels.

Though inflation took an upward trend in some countries, demand pressures were manifested largely in a widening of current account deficits. Inflows of private capital were also responsible for demand pressures. Private capital flows contributed to domestic macroeconomic pressures for three reasons. One, as countries had pursued capital account liberalization, borrowing overseas could more easily accommodate demand pressures. Two, East Asian countries became more appealing to investors as their growth rates increased. Three, asset price inflation was driven by private capital inflows. Consequently, capital flows to East Asian economies appeared to continue in tandem with domestic macroeconomic cycles, particularly in Indonesia, Thailand and Korea.[1] The macroeconomic policy mix utilized to deal with the overheating pressures and capital inflows in the 1990s added impetus for more inflows, and for the accumulation of short-term, unhedged external liabilities. Exchange rate policies played a major role in stimulating capital flows. The perception of reduced exchange rate risk suppressed incentives to hedge external borrowing and, moreover, created a bias toward short-term foreign currency borrowing.

Overall, the policy mix increased the incentives for unhedged external borrowing. During 1994-96, this policy mix was most prominent in the cases of Indonesia and Thailand and, consequently, short-term liabilities rose sharply in these two countries. To a large extent, the regulatory framework influenced the differences in incentives and possibilities to borrow within countries. For instance, in Indonesia, banks were provided limits in the amount of foreign exchange exposure they could assume and it was the corporate sector that borrowed large amounts offshore. In Korea and Thailand, non-bank financial institutions (NBFIs) had relatively no control to borrow overseas. In Malaysia, after the large borrowings in the early 1980s, both financial institutions and corporations were restricted in the amount to which they could take on foreign exchange exposures; thus, foreign claims were relatively nominal in mid-1997.

Financial systems in the crisis-affected countries generally did not perform well in intermediating capital.[2] These countries, especially Thailand that relied excessively on its banks, rather than foreign investment, were the most vulnerable. Incentives for excessive borrowing abroad arose from implicit government guarantees, high domestic funding costs, and the creation of offshore banking centers.

Foreign investors were partly responsible for the over-borrowing, as they did not always appropriately price risks, or undertake full evaluations of countries or individual borrowers. Spreads for non-sovereign borrowers in the East Asian countries, which were already lower than for other emerging markets, decelerated even quicker compared to borrowers from other emerging markets during the 1990s, and in late 1996 and early 1997 were often only slightly above those for long-term maturity loans to U.S. corporations. This decline in spreads was often followed by poor assessments of risk and performance; as late as May 1997, for example, investors were purchasing large amounts of short-term paper from Indonesian corporations with only a few days of due diligence.

The reinforcing impacts of high and increasing investment levels, vast private capital inflows and asset booms, together with the underlying shortcomings in financial systems, were responsible for the accumulation of a number of vulnerabilities, such as increased banking fragility, increased exposure to risky sectors, and increased borrowing short in foreign currency and lending long in domestic currency. These impacts not only reinforced macroeconomic policy, but they reinforced each other. Nonetheless, there were differences between countries that had paramount roles in both triggering the crisis and in the evolution of the crisis once it was under way.

Throughout East Asia, financial liberalization, rise in financial savings, and surge in capital inflows resulted in increases in monetary aggregates. In turn, as governments failed to acknowledge that monetary and credit growth, as well as capital inflows, were excessive, the growing liquidity and monetization of these economies brought about a generalized surge in bank and NBFI lending, although the amplitude and duration of these cycles, plus their apparent relationship with financial liberalization and the surge in capital inflows, differed from country to country. For instance, bank and non-bank credit to the private sector started going up at higher rates and on a sustained basis after the upsurge in capital inflows in Malaysia, the Philippines, and Thailand. This high growth rate hindered the banks' capacity to adequately evaluate risk. In Indonesia, on the other hand, the growth in bank and non-bank credit to the private sector was lower during the inflow period than in the years prior to the increase in foreign capital, partly due to the extensive financial reform it pursued before the inflow period.

Real estate lending was high, and banking sector exposure to real estate was more in countries with higher rates of credit growth proportional to GDP growth. This created risks, as both the real estate and securities markets were quite volatile in East Asia. Real estate price fluctuations during the 1990s were the highest in the Philippines and Malaysia, with a ratio of highest to lowest prices since inflows started of 3 and 2, respectively. Still, in both countries, vacancy rates in 1996 were relatively low at around 2 percent (and the banking sector exposure to real estate was low in the Philippines). In Thailand and Indonesia, the variability of real estate prices was lower, with high to low ratios of 1.25 and 1.32, respectively. However, vacancy rates in 1996 were quite high, at around 14 percent and increasing. In the East Asian countries, especially Thailand, the amount of construction at the end of 1996 already hinted towards a huge oversupply of real estate for the following two years.

Still, there were large differences among countries. For example, Korean banks did not have large property exposure. These banks, however, increased the share of bonds and other securities in their portfolios to almost 20 percent. Excluding the Philippines, the other crisis-stricken countries increased their exposure to bonds and other securities.

Since the late 1980s, banks' foreign exchange exposure increased significantly in Thailand, Malaysia, and the Philippines. Moreover, for Thailand and the Philippines, the stock of foreign liabilities of NBFIs soared quickly. In Indonesia, the upsurge of banks' foreign exchange exposure was significant through 1994, when there was a slight decline. During the same period, commercial banks in Korea did not reveal substantial increase in foreign exchange exposure, unlike Korean merchant banks and the corporate sector both of which raised foreign exchange exposures significantly.

Another vulnerability was brought about by maturity mismatches, especially on the external financing side. Initial levels of external debt in East Asia, with the exception of Indonesia, were quite low by international standards. However, during 1991-96, short-term external liabilities rose rapidly and a large portion of this borrowing was unhedged. In Thailand, the Philippines, Korea, and Malaysia, short-term foreign liabilities of banks rose quite quickly. Although Indonesian banks' short-term foreign liabilities did not rise rapidly, such liabilities of corporations did.

Prior to the crisis, the strongest indicator of vulnerability was the ratio of short-term external debt to external reserves. In June 1997, short-term debt in Korea, Thailand, and Indonesia exceeded external reserves by quite a large margin. This high ratio of short-term obligations to liquid foreign exchange assets made these countries much more susceptible to a potential run on their currencies, which arose from a loss of investor confidence.

The difficulties in the crisis-stricken economies emerged, however, in the banking systems. There were some shortcomings in their banking systems including: (a) low capital-adequacy ratios of banks; (b) inadequately designed and weakly enforced legal lending limits on single borrowers or group of related borrowers; (c) asset classification systems and provisioning rules for possible losses, which did not meet the international standards; (d) poor disclosure and transparency of bank operations; (e) lack of provisions for an exit policy of troubled financial institutions; and (f) weak supervision.

Weak governance of banks, normally affected directly or indirectly by government policies, added to the poor performance. An important shortcoming was the limited institutional development of banks. Much of the lending, for instance, was provided on a collateral basis, rather than on a cash-flow basis, thus obscuring the need to assess the profitability and riskiness of the underlying projects. Credit seemed to flow to borrowers with relationships to government or private bank owners and to favored sectors, rather than on the basis of projected cash flows, realistic sensitivity analysis, and recoverable collateral values.

Segments of the financial systems in some of these countries also exhibited a dismal performance. State-owned banks in Indonesia, finance companies in Thailand, and merchant banks in Korea revealed increasing signs of a deteriorating performance and increased risks. Fragmented financial system further abated competitiveness and stability. In Thailand, for example, finance companies could not increase deposits; they had to depend on higher cost of funds, which produced incentives to lend to more risky projects. The large number of weakly capitalized finance companies in Thailand and banks in Indonesia, for example, lowered the franchise value of financial institutions, thus weakening the incentives for prudent behavior. The competitiveness and institutional development of banking systems was hampered by the low domestic presence of foreign banks (Claessens and Glaessner, 1998).

These shortcomings did not suffice to put the financial system under immediate distress. All the crisis-affected economies had performed satisfactorily over the last decades despite these limitations. In the past, rapid economic growth and high domestic savings spared most of their banking systems from harmful consequences. Growing households' savings, in the form of bank deposits, by capital inflows, and generally high enterprise profitability allowed banks to roll over non-performing loans and continue to register bad assets on their books without any problems. Moreover, strong fiscal positions allowed governments to reassure investors and depositors that they could back up their banking systems. However, these financial sector shortcomings increased the risk of a financial crisis.

The process of financial liberalization without any adequate supervision further added to these risks. Domestic and external financial liberalization led to increased competition for credit-worthy borrowers, reducing the franchise value of banks and induced them to undertake more risky investment strategies. Rapidly growing NBFIs, often without adequate internal market and regulatory discipline, were an important avenue of competition for banks, especially in Korea and Thailand. Furthermore, as NBFIs were generally less regulated and subject to weaker supervision than banks, their growth, in terms of numbers and total credit expansion, directly exacerbated the system's fragility.

3.3 Evolution of the Crisis

The process of evolution of the crisis is best illustrated with the example of Thailand. In examining this process, it is important to touch upon the policy context in which the country experienced its worst crisis in many years. After the major devaluation of the exchange rate in 1984, the country had consistently maintained a stable exchange rate policy.

The economic boom witnessed by Thailand over a long period of time reassured it to implement far-reaching liberalization measures. Import duties were progressively lowered to a level of less than 20 percent by the end of 1996, compared with over 30 percent in 1994. In 1990, the country concurred to obligations under Article VIII of the Articles of Agreement of IMF under which it had to relax exchange controls on most current account transactions.

A number of measures impacting both current and capital account transactions were implemented under three rounds of liberalization of foreign exchange controls. The first round, in May 1990, allowed commercial banks to authorize foreign exchange transactions for trade-related activities without prior approval of the Central Bank, the Bank of Thailand, and increased the limit on foreign exchange purchase by domestic residents to facilitate transfers and travelling expenses. Moreover, commercial banks were allowed to remit funds for debt repayments, sale of stock, or liquidation of business within certain limits.

In April 1991, the second round conveyed a green signal to Thai residents to open foreign currency accounts provided the funds came from overseas. Exporters were permitted to take payments in baht from non-resident baht accounts, without prior approval from the Bank of Thailand, and utilize their export proceeds that came from overseas to service their external obligations without having to surrender them.

In February 1994, the third round raised the limit on outward transfer for direct investment by residents, raised the limit of bank notes to be taken to countries bordering Thailand (including Vietnam), ended the limit on travelling expenses and permitted residents to use foreign exchange proceeds originating overseas to service their external payments. However, some outbound investments including capital account transactions by Thai residents for outward portfolio and property investments, and outward FDI exceeding $10 million per investor a year continued to require approval from the concerned authorities.

The establishment of Bangkok International Banking Facility (BIBF) in 1993 was viewed as one of the principal measures in developing Thailand as a regional financial center. The BIBF was aimed to help enhance the capability of Thai financial institutions in international lending and other banking businesses and to provide a source for cheaper borrowing of foreign funds. The tasks allowed in the BIBF included deposit taking or borrowing in foreign currencies from overseas, lending in foreign currencies in Thailand and overseas, non-baht, cross-currency foreign exchange transactions, and investment banking activities such as arranging loan syndications and providing advisory services. By allowing out-in credits, the BIBF separated itself from offshore financial centers in other countries, which normally garner the benefits of the offshore business without exposing the local economy to the direct impact of foreign capital flows through these centers. For the expansion of the BIBF's operations, some tax privileges were provided as incentives.[3]

Interest rate liberalization began in 1989, with the relaxing of the ceiling on time deposits having maturity exceeding one year. The remaining ceilings on time deposits, savings deposits and loans for both commercial banks and finance companies were lifted in 1992. In the early 1990s, widening of the business scope of the different types of financial institutions was allowed. A process was also started to provide licences for establishing new banks and other financial institutions, both domestic and foreign.

Against the above policy context and the deterioration in some key economic indicators, the Thai currency, the baht, came under speculative attack in February and May 1997. Initially, official foreign exchange reserves were sold to protect the currency. In the process, the reserves fell down from about $39 billion in January 1997 to $32 billion in June 1997. Further, the Bank of Thailand sold over $23 billion of the reserves on the forward market. This quick depletion of reserves forced the bank to announce a float of the baht on 2 July 1997. Market sentiment deteriorated rapidly and prompted speculation and selling pressure on the other regional currencies, leading to an unprecedented decline in exchange rates by the end of 1997.

In parallel, the shortcoming of the financial sector had become quite clear. A case was the Bangkok Bank of Commerce Ltd., the control of which was taken over by the Ministry of Finance in May 1996, after it was on the verge of insolvency owing to very high levels of substandard debt and inadequate provisions for capital as well as loan loss. This was preceded by the collapse in early 1997 of Finance One Public Co. Ltd., one of the biggest finance companies in the country. As confidence in the financial system dropped considerably, borrowers faced increasing difficulties in rolling over short-term debt, outflows from finance companies and commercial banks increased and selling pressure on the stock exchange rose. Development in the stock market and in the currency market fed upon each other, and the subsequent liquidity crunch generated setbacks for the real economy through lowered access to credit for working capital, trade transactions and real estate purchases.

The general features of the process were similar for the other countries which were affected by the regional crisis.[4] There were, however, some dissimilarities in the economic conditions, policy details and institutional structures of individual economies.

3.4 Principal Factors

There have been two principal explanations placed forward for the advent of the crisis. One attributed it to poor economic fundamentals and policy inconsistencies, while the other argued that Asia was a victim to a financial panic, where negative sentiment became self-fulfilling.

The 'fundamentalist' view argued that the occurrence of the East Asian crisis was due to basic economic shortcomings. Advocates of this view asserted that a vague picture was illustrated by East Asia's strong macroeconomic indicators—low inflation, fiscal balance, low stock of government debt, high rates of domestic saving and investment—as depicted in Table 3.1. They maintained that in reality, East Asia's economies faced serious structural difficulties together with policy inconsistencies. They noted that warning signals existed; for instance, in Thailand the current account deficit was exceptionally large and rising quickly. Moreover, benign macroeconomic indicators, such as a healthy budget balance, could conceal real economic shortcoming. Many governments provided implicit guarantees to the banking system which often engaged in lending practices that were biased towards financially unsound borrowers. These guarantees led banks to lend carelessly. This, together with poor corporate governance in many of these economies, paved way for a large stock of nonperforming loans, thereby risking the banks' collapse (ADB, 1999).

Table 3.1: Macroeconomic Indicators of Selected Asian Economies

1990-1997 (in percent)

Economy	Growth Rate			Inflation Rate			Fiscal Balance/GDP		
	1990-1995	1996	1997	1990-1995	1996	1997	1990-1995	1996	1997
Korea	7.8	7.1	5.5	6.6	5.0	4.5	0.2	0.5	–1.4
Indonesia	8.0	7.8	4.9	8.7	7.9	6.6	0.2	0.2	0.0
Malaysia	8.9	8.6	7.7	3.7	3.5	4.0	–0.4	0.7	1.6
Philippines	2.3	5.8	5.2	10.6	9.1	6.0	–1.1	0.3	0.1
Singapore	8.6	6.9	7.8	2.7	1.4	2.0	9.4	6.8	3.3
Thailand	9.0	5.5	–0.4	5.0	5.9	5.6	3.2	2.4	–0.9
Hong Kong, China	5.0	4.5	5.3	9.3	6.3	5.9	1.6	2.2	6.5

Source: ADB (1999).

Economy	Saving/GDP			Investment/GDP			Current Account/GDP		
	1990-1995	1996	1997	1990-1995	1996	1997	1990-1995	1996	1997
Korea	35.6	33.7	33.1	36.8	38.4	35.0	–1.2	–4.7	–1.8
Indonesia	31.0	27.3	29.9	31.3	30.7	31.3	–2.5	–3.4	–1.4
Malaysia	36.6	42.6	43.8	37.5	41.5	42.0	–5.8	–5.0	–5.3
Philippines	16.6	18.5	20.3	22.4	23.1	23.8	–3.7	–4.7	–5.3
Singapore	47.0	51.2	51.8	34.9	35.3	37.4	0.6	15.4	15.4
Thailand	34.4	33.7	32.9	41.0	41.7	35.0	–3.9	–7.9	–2.0
Hong Kong, China	33.6	30.7	31.8	29.6	32.1	35.4	(–)	(–)	(–)

(–) : Not Available

Source: ADB (1999).

On the other hand, the panic interpretation attributed the major reason for the crisis to the self-fulfilling pessimism of international lenders. This argument took the crisis as a classic bank run. In a bank run, if enough investors are unexpectedly apprehended with panic and need immediate payment, then financial intermediaries are compelled to liquidate long-term assets at a huge loss. In the classic model of a panic, the central bank can limit such a bank run by performing the role of lender of last resort and providing liquidity to the market. However, in the international version of a bank run, if a country's exchange rate is fixed and foreign exchange reserves are limited compared to short-term external debt, as was the case in some of the crisis-affected countries, there is no mechanism for stopping panic. Short-term external debt in Indonesia, Korea, and Thailand exceeded international reserves immediately before the crisis, and indeed, for more than two years before the crisis. Table 3.2 shows the short-term external debt and international reserves prior to the crisis.

Table 3.2: Short-term External Debt and International Reserves Prior to the Crisis

(Second Quarter of 1997)

Country	Short-term Debt (In US$ billion)	International Reserves (In US$ billion)	Debt-reserve Ratio
Indonesia	34.66	20.34	1.70
Korea	70.18	34.07	2.06
Malaysia	16.27	26.59	0.61
Philippines	8.29	9.78	0.85
Thailand	45.57	31.36	1.45

Source: ADB (1999).

The spectacular economic record of the East Asian economies prior to the crisis does not corroborate with the fundamentalist views. However, a closer examination clearly reveals that these countries' economic success was built on a specific type of economic strategy that focused on export promotion, centralized coordination of production activities, and implicit government guarantees of private investment projects, along with close operational relationship and interlinked ownership between banks and firms. This strategy allowed firms to rely heavily on bank credit. By international standards, firms in crisis-stricken countries were highly leveraged. For example, in Korea and Thailand, the average debt-to-equity ratios in 1996 exceeded 200 percent. In Indonesia and the Philippines, debt-to-equity ratios were lower, but still high by international standards.

For many years, financial systems of most East Asian countries stayed relatively closed. Foreign borrowing was restricted and capital inflows were controlled. These controls made sure that the region's financial sectors were immune from external shocks despite their domestic fragility. Moreover, controls prohibited domestic fragility from being transformed into external vulnerability in the form of short-term, unhedged foreign debt. However, this situation did not prevail during the 1990s. As international capital markets were gradually opened and domestic markets were deregulated, supervision and regulatory oversight did not improve in tandem.

The 1990s was also a period of a sharp expansion in foreign borrowing. While East Asian companies maintained their strong preference in favor of debt financing, foreign debt financing became more important, as depicted in Table 3.3, for corporate debt composition in selected East Asian economies in 1996. The pegged exchange rate eliminated exchange risks in borrowing in dollars. Likewise, with interest rates low in advanced countries, international investors were searching for higher yields elsewhere. At the same time, there was growing optimism about East Asia's prospects. Between 1991 and 1996 overall borrowing doubled in Malaysia and Thailand and grew by one third in Korea (ADB, 1999). The fundamentalist interpretation of the crisis links this optimism among foreign investors to their belief that the borrowing was finally guaranteed, either by East Asian governments or by international institutions. The panic interpretation considers the optimism as rational, based on the correct judgment that these economies were fundamentally sound.

Table 3.3: Composition of Corporate Debt, 1996

(in percent)

Country	Foreign Debt		Domestic Debt	
	Short-term	Long-term	Short-term	Long-term
Indonesia	20.5	19.6	31.4	28.5
Korea	29.4	17.0	27.7	25.8
Malaysia	32.1	11.0	35.7	21.2
Philippines	19.7	21.3	25.5	33.5
Thailand	29.6	12.3	32.0	26.1

Note: Data are drawn from a sample of 5,550 Asian firms.

Source: Claessens, Djankov and Lang (1998).

Even though particular features differed, a pattern of rising vulnerability to external shocks was witnessed in all the East Asian economies prior to the crisis. One, short-term borrowing to finance long-term projects became more important, especially in Korea, Malaysia, and Thailand. This led to a sizable maturity mismatch in the balance sheets of local financial institutions. Two, domestic banks provided credit to domestic firms in local currency, while borrowing short-term in foreign currencies without hedging. This resulted in a significant currency denomination mismatch. Three, the easy availability of credit stimulated investment in very risky assets. The credit boom was transformed into bubbles in real estate and property in some countries. In other countries, financial resources were geared towards overinvestment in narrowly specialized industries such as electronics or large, prestigious projects with vague benefits. These poor and risky investments, subsequently, worsened the quality of the portfolios of domestic financial institutions, thereby exacerbating the risk of panics and subsequent crises.

During the first half of 1997, capital inflows did not slow down, but took the shape of short-term, interbank loans that could be easily and readily taken out and could depend on formal guarantees in the interbank markets. Nonetheless, once the crisis struck, international banks suddenly discontinued lending and began to recall their loans. A huge amount of private foreign capital left the region in the second half of 1997. Between them, Indonesia, Korea, Malaysia, Philippines, and Thailand obtained a net capital inflow of about $76 billion in 1996, but suffered a net capital outflow of around $36 billion in 1997. This implied a difference of approximately $112 billion, or about 12 percent of the countries' combined GDP. Commercial banks withdrew about $26 billion from the crisis-stricken countries in 1997, after advancing them about $63 billion in 1996.[5]

The abruptness and pace with which capital flight took place in the region in the second half of 1997 imparts recognition to the panic interpretation of the crisis. However, it was the region's structural shortcomings that initially build up the vulnerability to the crisis.

3.5 Other Factors

Although their exchange rates denoted flexibility, the currencies of the crisis-affected economies had been closely pegged to the U.S. dollar. Moreover, these economies were following stringent monetary policies with high interest rates to contain demand pressures and maintain inflation under control. One cardinal assumption of international economics is that a country cannot simultaneously peg its exchange rate and undertake an independent monetary policy to achieve domestic objectives. With capital controls, the situation is even more intricate. Banks and corporate sectors in these economies could access the international markets as they chose low cost loans in U.S. dollars or Japanese yen to the high cost of local currency loans, given the implicit exchange rate guarantee. Consequently, foreign liabilities rose. The short-term external debts became particularly troublesome when foreign lenders requested for repayments. Foreign exchange reserves were used as long as possible to meet these repayment demands, while keeping exchange rates unchanged. However, with the massive capital outflows, the floating and market-determined valuation of these currencies became inevitable. As contagion took hold, the crisis extended from Thailand to other East Asian economies, after which their currencies were floated.

With the high levels of foreign indebtedness in financial institutions and corporates, these financial institutions and corporates were in a position where they were not able to service their debts at the steeply depreciated exchange rates. All of a sudden, the major parts of these sectors became technically insolvent. The financial sectors virtually bursted from the flood of bad debts. Letters of credit for confirmed export orders could not be opened and working capital was absent as banks unnecessarily attempted to shore up their balance sheets to satisfy their capital adequacy requirements. Banks normally had their doors open, but often only deposit account services were provided. Moreover, with high short-term interest rates, banks suffered losses as they funded their outstanding term loans with very costly short-term funds. Financial sectors became, to a great degree, non-operational and without financial services, there was a sharp drop in business sector operations.

The financial crisis in East Asia was clearly not the upshot of excessive government expenditures owing to the good record of budgetary control in the region. Thailand had budget surpluses during the 1990-96 period while both Korea and Indonesia had surpluses in the years immediately prior to the crisis after small deficits in the early 1990s. The 'old-style' crises arose on the current account of the balance of payments while the 'new-style' crises (which first occurred in East Asia) originated on the capital account. From a crisis rooted in trade imbalances, there was a transformation with the East Asian financial crisis to a crisis rooted in sharp reversals of capital flows. Instead of macroeconomic weaknesses paving the way for unsustainable trade and current account deficits, an abrupt loss in confidence in East Asia resulted in a reversal of capital inflows. These led to a decline in exchange rates and domestic asset values that subsequently brought down large parts of the banking and corporate sectors.

Competition between the over-guaranteed and under-regulated banks inspired bankers to provide credit on the basis of a project's expected return in ideal circumstances, resulting in excessive capital inflows, over-investment and asset price bubbles. The financial sectors in East Asia were not properly regulated and they were implicitly over-guaranteed as substantiated by the actual guarantees provided by the related governments once the crisis struck.

East Asian banking systems also seemed to be well protected by governments in the belief that they would not witness any difficulties. Ironically such protection only undermined these systems. Banking systems were provided protection by governments or central banks through restrictions on the entry of new banks, either domestic or foreign, and restrictions on the exit of weak, non-performing banks through mergers or bankruptcies with financial assistance for failing institutions. Such approaches only helped in weakening competition, weakening governance by further sharing risk, and lessening the resilience of the banking sector.

3.6 IMF's Role and Criticisms

Prior to the onset of the East Asian crisis, the IMF had warned Thailand of impending problems, but the government ignored the warning and undertook no measures. The IMF's staff also cautioned about financial sector weaknesses in the countries that were subsequently affected by the crisis. At the same time, the IMF was unable in foreseeing the severity of the contagion impacts emanating from the crisis.

The financing packages arranged to support the crisis-stricken countries were quite striking: $36 billion for Indonesia, $58 billion for Korea, and $17 billion for Thailand (Lane, 1999). However, all of the money was not available, especially at the outset, to respond to market pressures. This was because the IMF support was phased, that is, made available in tranches, over the life of the programs. The aim was to ensure that the related authorities had a continuing incentive to stick to the adjustment policies agreed under the program, but it did lower the authorities' ability to counter immediate market pressures. Again, a portion of the bilateral money promised to Indonesia and Korea was never disbursed.

All three IMF-supported programs demanded a substantial rise in interest rates in order to end the downward spiral of currency depreciation. These programs also insisted on forceful action to put the financial system on a sounder footing, strengthening financial sector regulation and supervision, raising transparency, and opening East Asian markets to foreign investors. These strategies were required to restore confidence and support a resumption of growth and included reforms tailored to address the particular shortcomings of each country. A glimpse of these strategies pertaining to Indonesia, Republic of Korea and Thailand is provided in Appendix 3.2.

There were two major constituents in the IMF's economic strategy. The first one focused on macroeconomic policy, the constituent of which was to be tighter monetary policy. Higher interest rates were aimed at defending the exchange rates, and so restricting (or reversing) the capital outflows. Tighter fiscal policy was aimed at supporting current account adjustment and supplying the funds required to bailout the sick financial institutions. The second, complementary, constituent was structural reform. The IMF called for serious reform of the region's banking systems, the breakup of monopolies, the abolishment of barriers to trade, and substantial improvements in corporate transparency. It considered structural reforms as essential for a long-term solution to East Asia's financial crisis.

Financial support was also provided by the World Bank, the Asian Development Bank (ADB), and governments in Asia, Europe, and the U.S. The basic strategy was to: (i) assist crisis-stricken countries to rebuild their official reserves; (ii) buy time for policy adjustments and reforms to restore confidence and stabilize economies; and (iii) reduce any lasting disruption to countries' relations with external creditors.[6]

A few critics challenged the IMF's persistence on sweeping structural reforms in East Asian economies. They viewed that the IMF went far ahead of its mandate of ensuring prudent macroeconomic policies. Instead, it was intervening too much in the domestic affairs of sovereign governments by demanding large-scale restructuring in the corporate and financial sector, along with improvements in governance, labor markets, and competition policy.

The IMF's defendants argued that these critics were unaware of the actual facts of the crisis. If careless monetary and fiscal expansion was not at the root of the crisis, as those who consider the IMF as being too intrusive also recognize, building up a response focusing on these areas did not make any sense. However, if, as is accepted, structural weaknesses in corporate governance and the financial system was the factor behind East Asia's troubles, then the IMF's loan programs would have had very little chance of success if they had not addressed structural reforms. Supplying large-scale financial assistance to support the region's currencies would have been unwise if the major cause of the problem was left unaddressed. Continued financial and corporate sector shortcomings would have weakened macroeconomic policy, foreign investment would have continued to move out of the country, and the IMF's final objective—a quick return to economic growth—would have been impossible.

While much of the criticism of the IMF was linked to its policies for East Asia, some criticized the very existence of IMF support. This argument was based on the concept of moral hazard which implies that investors and borrowers behave indiscreetly since they believe they will be bailed out if their investments become sour. The IMF loans, according to some critics, exacerbated moral hazard in two ways: they forgave governments from the impact of profligate policies, thus encouraging them to continue the profligacy in the future, and they rewarded irresponsible investors. Because the IMF's loans to the crisis-stricken countries were unusually substantial, the critics contended that they put a dangerous precedent that would raise moral hazard worldwide.

Though multibillion dollar support packages faced some risk of changing investors' incentives, there were three reasons that showed that the critics overstated the moral hazard argument. One, many investors in East Asia, both foreign and domestic, suffered huge losses. Investors had witnessed the value of their investments reduced to a third or a quarter of their pre-crisis value. Two, it was hard to imagine that governments totally agreed to the tough conditions that IMF imposed on them. Many governments that seek the assistance of the IMF later lose power, as they are forced to execute politically unpopular measures. Three, if the IMF had not intervened, the costs would have been extremely high. Investors would have exited even more quickly, countries would have been forced to default on their debts, and the region could have fallen into an even more severe crisis.

There were two problems that made it difficult to give a clear assessment of the IMF's policies. The first related to the insoluble problem of the counterfactual. Knowing exactly what would have happened if the IMF had proposed a different approach is impossible. The second difficulty was that the IMF's targets and approaches changed with the passage of time. As the situation in East Asia worsened, the IMF relaxed its approach and called for less fiscal contraction. For instance, in Indonesia, it relaxed its earlier condition of a budget surplus in 1997 to permit for a sizable budget deficit. The crucial question was whether these changes in policy were an implicit recognition of initial misjudgments by the IMF, or whether they just indicated a flexible response to changing conditions.

3.7 Lessons Drawn

A number of lessons can be drawn from the East Asian crisis. Policy responses to preclude the emergence of financial crises in the future should include, among others, developing suitable macroeconomic policies, enhancing export competitiveness, choosing the right exchange rate system, appropriately restructuring the financial and corporate sectors, effectively regulating and supervising banks and defining the role for the government, establishing an international lender of last resort, carefully supervising and regulating international capital flows, defining the responsibility of the private creditors, and monitoring vulnerabilities effectively. These issues are examined at length in the undergoing paragraphs.

The crisis has shown that in devising and implementing macroeconomic policies, one has to consider their impact on the health of the financial system. In this respect, there are three important lessons that can be extracted from Chile's experience in the late 1970s (Zahler, 1996). One, macroeconomic volatility should be reduced through coherent and consistent macroeconomic policies, as macroeconomic instability increases the vulnerability of bank debtors, leads to ill-suited and flawed asset risk evaluation by banks, and ultimately makes the banking system more fragile. Two, policies should favor flexibility so as to distribute macroeconomic shocks among different markets and avoid focusing the impacts of a shock in a particular market in a way that would prove unbearable and unsustainable. Three, the appropriate speed at which to liberalize the domestic financial sector relative to the foreign financial sector or the appropriate sequence in which to open trade and to liberalize the financial sector are not the same in every country or in a single country under different initial conditions. If reforms are not properly sequenced and paced, the condition may end up worse than it was initially.

In this context, capital account liberalization should proceed cautiously, in an orderly way. The benefits of capital account liberalization and increased capital flows have to be measured against the possibility of a crisis and its cost. For FDI and long-term capital inflows, the balance of expected benefits over the costs linked to financial crises is positive, and developing countries need to go for openness. However, for more volatile debt portfolio and interbank short-term debt flows, there are more related risks of financial crisis and uncertainty about benefits. Tighter prudential regulations on banks and, where the domestic regulatory system is weak, prohibition on more volatile short-term flows could support in lowering the risk of crisis.

There are other lessons that can be drawn. One, countries need to continue with efforts to enhance their export competitiveness through technological upgrading improvements in the quality of human resources and increase in the domestic value-added component of exports, including by lowering the import intensity. The main justification is to ensure that legitimate import requirements are primarily financed by export earnings, rather than short-term private credit.

Two, the East Asian crisis depicted that pegged, but adjustable, exchange rates were hard to sustain in a world of increasing capital mobility. Before long they are likely to be tested by a speculative attack, compelling high interest rates and budget cuts. The crisis also supported another traditional claim against fixed, but adjustable, exchange rates: by developing an illusion of permanent currency stability, they strengthen the incentive for financial institutions and firms to borrow from abroad without hedging.

Three, from the experience of the East Asian crisis, the policy recommendations to support the development of the financial system and improve corporate governance became clear-cut: (a) fixing accounting, auditing, and disclosure standards to raise the flow of information, and enhancing efficiency by improving the quality of investment, reducing misallocations, resolving mistakes quickly, and strengthening business risk assessment and the accountability of managers to shareholders; (b) developing the legal infrastructure—bankruptcy laws, debt workout processes, implementation of collateral and guarantees—to write and enforce contracts confidently and to protect and balance the interests of creditors, shareholders, and managers, thus developing a credit culture in which trust and expectations of repayment transactions costs are reduced; and (c) banning connected lending practices.

Four, the crisis exposed serious weaknesses in the financial sectors of many of the affected economies. These weaknesses concerned not only the operations of the individual financial institutions but also the regulatory and supervisory regimes overseeing them.[7]

Thus, in this context, inadequate regulation and supervision have been the most acknowledged source of vulnerability in developing countries' banking systems. Most industrial countries follow the "Core Principles for Effective Supervision" of the Basel Committee in the design of banking regulation and supervision to reduce vulnerability of the financial system. Policymakers need also to apply these principles which should be the declared minimum norm in the banking and financial sector.

As government generally plays an instrumental role in the banking sector in developing countries, this creates serious conflicts, especially moral hazard problems that are a prime factor in risky lending. Essential reforms in this area include: (a) limiting the government's role in directly running and managing banks which could imply privatization of banks, which has to be handled scrupulously, especially in terms of pricing, treatment of risks, capital adequacy, and management; (b) reducing the government's direct participation in allocation of credit and in providing guarantees to commercial enterprises so as to boost up market-oriented banking behavior; and (c) developing a formal deposit insurance scheme to deal with the negative externalities that individual failures may have on the rest of the banking system.

Five, the crisis showed that adequate provision of liquidity was very crucial for pre-empting the crisis, minimizing contagion and mitigating negative impact. In this respect, there were calls for an international lender of last resort (ILLR). Currently, a true ILLR does not exist.[8] As an institution with a mandate to provide balance of payments assistance to its member countries, IMF acts as the *de facto* ILLR. During the East Asian crisis, it provided liquidity assistance after countries were hit by the crisis, subject to fulfilment of its conditions. Moreover, due to the scarcity of resources at its disposal, IMF played the role of more as an organizer than as a provider of funds.

The establishment of an ILLR lender of resort could generate a host of advantages. A country may be put in danger with deep financial difficulties through no mistake of its own. For example, an unexpected drop in demand of its exports or changes in interest rates in capital exporting countries could result in massive capital outflows and depletion of reserves. The provision of liquidity in advance could pre-empt a crisis generated by short-term investors and creditors moving out of a country together. An ILLR would also be able to supply reserves to developing countries threatened by speculative attacks and thus avert a collapse of the currency.[9]

Six, it was learnt from the crisis that as most of the capital inflow in East Asian countries affected by the crisis arose from private sources, the responsibility of private sector creditors has to be suitably defined in handling issues of indebtedness. For any orderly, durable and equitable debt workout, it is important that some principles are globally agreed upon to avoid placing the burden wholly on debtor countries. In these principles, bank debt need not have any seniority in claims compared with, for instance, bonds or debentures.[10]

Moreover, attention should be accorded to a mutually satisfactory adjustment of claims. A number of formulas can be employed: roll-overs; conversion of debt into longer-term securities; reduction in its face value; reducing interest rates; or, for instance, a temporary standstill on debt servicing. Any standstill should be subject to validation by an international institution with the aim to bypass any harsh judgment by market participants and loss of confidence.

Seven, the East Asia crisis disclosed weaknesses in the coverage, frequency, and timeliness of information available for evaluating vulnerabilities. Before the crisis struck, and for many weeks after, the amount of foreign liabilities to which the countries were exposed were not precisely known. Uncertainty about short-term debt and foreign exchange reserves exacerbated the financial panic. Questions also arose about the disclosure of information and transparency of international financial institutions themselves. Accordingly, improvements are required on information and disclosure at all levels (private sector, national authorities and international financial institutions), and international standards should be applied scrupulously and progressively over time, taking into account constraints and costs.

Eight, though warning indicators are unlikely to predict crises, particularly their timing, they can provide timely and accurate information about severe problems so that policymakers can take the necessary actions. Two methods are generally employed. The first one is the signals method, which determines the characteristic and abnormal behavior of a set of variables, that is, leading indicators, preceding crises, relative to tranquil periods. The indicators that predict the actual crises and produce the minimum false alarms are taken as leading indicators. The second one is the regression method, which examines statistical significance of various indicators in models of crisis determination. Warning indicators of vulnerability generally provide positive signals for many variables simultaneously. There does not appear to be a uniform, well-defined set of indicators, however. Country conditions seem to be crucial in determining the importance of specific indicators.[11]

Finally, focus should also be accorded to the major vulnerability indicators of a currency crisis including exchange rates appreciation, international illiquidity, as computed by the ratio of short-term liabilities to reserves, money stock to reserves, or foreign assets to liabilities (of banks), and lending booms financed by foreign borrowing. Other important indicators are slower GDP and export growth, higher foreign interest rates, worsening terms of trade, a decline in equity prices, and a banking crisis (Kaminsky and Reinhart, 1997).

However, the indicator that is generally linked with currency rises is the size of the current account deficit. In general, empirical work has not been able to find current account deficits themselves in predicting a crisis, excluding one which shows that the ratios of current account deficit to GDP and to investment is one the of principal indicators of currency crises (Goldstein and Reinhart, 1998). Still, current account deficits are important in assessing vulnerability if supplemented by analysis of the causal factors. Large or fast-increasing deficits are always needed to be monitored, as they normally indicate increasing capital inflows. Deficits should also be carefully monitored if spending is on consumption rather than investment, especially in the tradeables sector, since there is presumption of lower risks because of faster growth of GDP and exports.

Appendix 3.1: East Asian Financial Crisis: Chronology of Important Events

1997	Events
2 July	Thailand devalues the baht and declares a managed float of the currency. The value of the baht drops by as much as 20 percent. The Thai government requests 'technical assistance' from the IMF. The Philippines intervenes to defend its peso.
8 July	Malaysia's central bank intervenes to defend its currency, the ringgit.
11 July	The Philippine peso is devalued. Indonesia widens its trading band for the rupiah in order to discourage speculators.
18 July	IMF approves an extension of credit to the Philippines of US$ 1.1 billion.
24 July	The Singapore dollar starts a gradual decline.
5 Aug.	Thailand agrees to adopt tough economic measures proposed by the IMF. The Thai government closes 42 ailing finance companies and imposes tax hikes.
13-14 Aug.	The Indonesian rupiah comes under severe pressure. Indonesia abolishes its system of managing its exchange rate through the use of a band.
20 Aug.	IMF announces US$ 17.2 billion support package for Thailand.
28 Aug.	Asian stock markets plunge. Manila is down 9.3 percent, Jakarta 4.5 percent.
4 Sep.	The peso, ringgit, and rupiah continue to fall.
20-23 Oct.	The Hong Kong dollar comes under speculative attack; the government aggressively defends its currency. The Hong Kong stock market and other stock markets also take sharp falls.
28 Oct.	The value of the Korean won drops as investors sell Korean stocks.

31 Oct.	The IMF agrees to a loan package for Indonesia that ultimately swells to US$ 40 billion. In return, the government closes 16 financially insolvent banks and promises wide-ranging reforms.
25 Nov.	At the APEC summit, leaders of the 18 Asia Pacific economies endorse a framework to cope with financial crises.
3 Dec.	Republic of Korea and IMF agree on US$ 57 billion support package.
25 Dec.	IMF and others provide US$ 10 billion in loans to Republic of Korea.
1998	
6 Jan.	Indonesia unveils new budget that does not appear to meet IMF austerity conditions.
8 Jan.	IMF and Republic of Korea agree to a 90-day rollover of short-term debt.
12 Jan.	Asia's largest private investment bank, the Hong Kong-based Peregrine Investments Holdings, files for liquidation.
15 Jan.	IMF and Indonesia sign a new loan deal agreeing to eliminate the country's monopolies and state subsidies.
29 Jan.	Republic of Korea and 13 international banks agree to convert US$ 24 billion in short-term debt, due in March 1998, into government-backed loans.
31 Jan.	Republic of Korea orders 10 of 14 ailing merchant banks to close.
9 Mar.	IMF announces that it is delaying a US$ 3 billion installment of its US$ 40 billion loan package to Indonesia, citing President Suharto's unwillingness to implement his side of the deal.

8 Apr.	Indonesia and the IMF reach a third pact in six months for a bailout. Both sides make concessions: the IMF withdraws its mandate that the government dismantle its subsidies of food and fuel while the government agrees to close more insolvent banks. IMF Deputy Director Stanley Fischer declares "the worst of the crisis is over."
4 May	IMF resumes a stalled lending program to Indonesia, approving a payment of US$ 1 billion.
12 June	Japan declares that its economy is in a recession for the first time in 23 years.
25 June	Indonesia and the IMF announce a fourth agreement. The IMF agrees to restore subsidies for food and fuel and provide another US$ 4 billion to US$ 6 billion for basic necessities.

Sources: Nanto (1998) and *Frontline* (date not available).

Appendix 3.2: IMF Conditionality for Selected Countries

	Indonesia	Republic of Korea	Thailand
Macroeconomic policy framework	Public sector: tight budget; subsidies reduced or re-moved; reduction of tariffs; revoking special tax, credit and custom privileges to 'national projects'; divestiture of state enterprises; inclusion of non-budgetary revenues into the state budget; cancellation of some government financed or guaranteed infrastructure projects.	Public sector: tight budget; broadening of VAT base; selective increases in income and corporate taxes; cuts in government expenditure.	Public sector: tight budget, VAT increases; subsidies reduced or removed; reduced government expenditure except for health and education; divestiture of state enterprises.
	Monetary sector: independence of the central bank; tight monetary policy, flexible exchange rate.	Monetary sector: tight monetary policy; flexible exchange rate; independence of central bank.	Monetary sector: tight monetary policy; flexible exchange rate.
	Macroeconomic targets for 1998 (as in the renewed agreement, January 1998): Inflation: 20 percent, Growth: 0 percent, Budget: 1 percent deficit of GDP, Current account deficit: 2.2 percent of GDP, Official reserves: 5.2 months of imports.	Macroeconomic targets for 1998: Inflation: 25 percent, Growth: 2.5 percent, Budget: 0.2 percent surplus of GDP, Current account deficit: 2.3 percent of GDP, Official reserves: not available.	Macroeconomic targets for 1998: Inflation: 5.0 percent, Growth: 3.5 percent, Budget: 1 percent surplus of GDP, revised to 1 or 2 percent deficit, Current account deficit: 3.0 percent of GDP, Official reserves: 4 months of imports.

Structural policies	Financial sector: closure of troubled banks; comprehensive financial restructuring, strengthening the regulatory framework; deposit guarantee for small depositors; no government guarantee for private non-financial companies, domestic or foreign.	Financial sector: comprehensive restructuring of financial sector; improving accounting and disclosure rules in accordance with international standards; recapitalizing financial institutions; establishing an agency to consolidate the supervisory functions of financial institutions.	Financial sector: suspension and restructuring of unviable financial institutions; strengthening the capital base of financial institutions; improving accounting standards and disclosure rules; strengthening the supervisory framework; removal of unconditional financial support to insolvent institutions.
	Trade sector: removal of state regulated or sponsored monopolies and cartels; a separate privatization board to manage corporatization; abolition of restrictions on marketing arrangements.	Trade sector: trade and competition; elimination of trade-related subsidies, removal of restrictive import licensing, promotion of labor market flexibility; further reduction of restrictions on FDI.	Trade sector: enhancing competitiveness in the export sector through increased emphasis on education and training.
	Social safety net: public expenditure on health, education and social expenditure programmes not to be cut; special assistance programmes for poor villages to be increased.	Social safety net: strengthening the employment insurance system; establishment of private job placement and temporary employment agencies.	Social safety net: expenditure on essential areas, such as health and education, to be protected from cuts.

Source: ESCAP (1998).

NOTES

1. Korea denotes Republic of Korea throughout the text.
2. As mentioned earlier in this study, the crisis-affected economies of East Asia specifically refer to Indonesia, Korea and Thailand and, to lesser extent to Malaysia and the Philippines.
3. All in all, the establishment of BIBF produced two major changes in the structure of Thailand's balance of payments and external debt. The first was the rapid growth of offshore borrowing by Thai residents through BIBF. This growth implied

both a switch in new borrowing to BIBF and shifts in capital inflows from other types of financing to BIBF. The second was a sharp shortening of Thailand's external debt maturity partly due to a change in the way in which BIBF banks made funds available to local borrowers (Krongkaew, 1999).

4. A brief chronology of important events during the East Asian financial crisis is depicted in Appendix 3.1.
5. These data are based on ADB (1999).
6. According to Park *et al.* (2017), the mix of policies differed from country to country, but generally included measures to clear up the balance sheets, rehabilitate weak financial systems, and improve competitiveness.
7. While on the one hand, the intermediating entities were unaware of, or unable to measure precisely, the fundamental risk of many of the investment and lending decisions they had made, they did not have the capital strength to absorb the losses that were then incurred on the other. Supervisory and regulatory authorities were also very slow in executing their tasks properly, whether with respect to banking regulation or capital market supervision, but particularly in allowing a lack of transparency to thrive.
8. While no thorough mechanism has been executed, it was in late 1997 that the IMF introduced the supplemental reserve facility (SRF). This was aimed at making large short-term loans with policy conditions at penalty rates during crises. So far, however, only Korea, Russia and Brazil have used the SRF.
9. The major concern, however, is fear of moral hazard, since access to a liquidity facility may lead countries to choose bolder policies with less liquidity self-protection (for instance, lower reserves) and, when there is a liquidity crisis, to opt to incur debt from the ILLR to avoid default on private debts and preserve creditworthiness (Calomris, 2003).
10. It should be remembered that in the East Asian crisis most of the borrowers were *de facto* bankrupt. Had they gone into liquidation, banks would have recuperated only a small fraction of their original loan amounts and that too, after a long delay.
11. In this respect, many studies have revealed that traditional indicators of vulnerability, especially those associated with indebtedness, fiscal policy, sovereign risk ratings, and interest spreads, have not been successful in sending useful warning indicators of currency crises.

Chapter 4

Global Financial Crisis

4.1 Introduction

The historical perspective on the decades leading up to the GFC shows that the global economy was by no means as stable as indicated by many observers. Indeed, the GFC was the greatest economic shock since the Great Depression of the 1930s. The crisis was largely unanticipated and because of its complex roots, it mystified policymakers and economists as it struck first at banks and companies, and then economies across the globe. However, some countries were more impacted than others owing to differences in initial conditions (state of economy, labor market, fiscal space, and institutional framework, among others) and exposure to direct and indirect impact of the crisis through the credit and trade channels.

The GFC began in the summer of 2007, though the full impact was not experienced till the bankruptcy of the investment bank, Lehman Brothers, in September 2008. The next few years saw massive employment losses and contraction in the GDP of many countries in the West as well as in the developing world. Hence, what began off with the subprime mortgage crisis quickly transformed into a full-blown crisis of historic proportions and ultimately resulted in a fundamental review of financial regulation, both in economies in the epicenter of the crisis and those on the periphery.

4.2 Origin of the Crisis

After the burst of the 'dotcom' bubble in 2000 along with the 2001 terror attacks on the U.S., the U.S. and most other advanced countries embarked on the path of sustained expansionary economic policies to ward off recession. The Federal Reserve, for example, reduced its discount rate no less than 27 times between 2001 and 2003. Low interest rates, facilitated by the massive trade surpluses which China and other countries utilized to purchase U.S. treasury bonds, inspired rapid growth in credit. Subsequent increases in house prices further fuelled credit growth, particularly *via* mortgage lending. In the U.S., subprime market mortgage lending to households without the essential means to repay loans was quite high: about US$ 1.3 trillion was lent in subprime mortgages (Lin, 2008). U.S. mortgage lenders, primarily Fanny Mae and Freddie Mac, securitized these subprime loans, which were then sold as assets throughout the financial system. They were able to issue and securitize these bad loans owing to a combination of insufficient regulation and financial innovation. The latter made it difficult for other institutions to evaluate the risks of these securitized mortgages and resulted in increased subprime mortgages.

By July 2007, rising defaults on mortgages and increasing numbers of foreclosures in the U.S. indicated that the subprime market was in crisis. House prices and financial stock prices began to plunge which reduced the value of household wealth. The solvency of Fanny Mae and Freddie Mac along with a number of international financial institutions was threatened by these defaults and the fall in house and stock prices. The U.S. Government nationalized Fanny Mae and Freddie Mac on 7 September 2008. Then, on 15 September 2008, Lehman Brothers with US$ 639 billion filed for bankruptcy, which was the largest in the country's history.

The downfall of Lehman Brothers sent a wave of panic around the global financial markets with banks practically discontinuing lending to each other. The risk premium on interbank borrowing soared to 5 percent, whereas typically it was almost zero. Even though the authorities rushed to inject liquidity into financial markets, the damage had already been done. The risk premium on corporate bonds surged even more exceeding 6 percent (Naude, 2009). Large capital expenditure projects were shelved, the corporate sector virtually discontinued borrowing, trade credit was difficult to obtain and, with dwindling demand, especially for investment goods and manufacturing durables like cars, trade volumes collapsed. The outcome was that the GFC witnessed the largest and sharpest drop in global economic activity of the modern era.

When the U.S. House of Representatives on 29 September 2008 first declined a US$ 700 billion bailout proposal for the financial firms adversely affected by the credit crunch, Wall Street's Dow Index saw its largest one-day point loss in history.

Banks in Europe were soon impacted because of their exposure to the U.S. financial markets. On 8 October 2008 the U.K. Government recapitalized eight of the country's banks along with an agreement amongst the euro zone countries on 15 October on injecting further capital into distressed banks and providing guarantees for interbank loans, at the cost to the taxpayer exceeding US$ 1.3 trillion.

The above analysis depicts that the anatomy of the crisis was quite simple: easy credit, bad loans, weak regulation and supervision of complex financial instruments, debt defaulting, insolvency of major financial institutions, a loss of credibility and trust, and financial panic and mass selling-off of stocks as well as a hoarding of cash by banks and individuals. Due to the interconnectedness of financial markets, especially among the developed countries, the panic spread quickly, triggering a widespread credit crunch and sharp drops in consumption, investment and trade in all of the G7 countries initially.[1]

4.3 Causes and Resemblances with Other Crises

Some of the factors that were responsible for the GFC were also, to a large extent, responsible for the crises of the earlier episodes. These included: (a) rapid surges in asset prices; (b) credit booms; (c) a dramatic expansion in marginal loans; and (d) regulation and supervision that failed to keep up with developments (Claessens *et al.*, 2010).

In the GFC, it was the house prices that sharply rose prior to the meltdown, including in Iceland, Ireland, Spain, the United

Kingdom, the United States, and other markets that subsequently ran into problems. The patterns of house price increases were suggestive of those in earlier major crisis occurrences. The overall size of the housing booms and their dynamics—including house prices rising over 30 percent in the five years preceding the crisis and peaking just before the beginning of the crisis—was analogous to developments that preceded previous banking crises in advanced economies (Reinhart and Rogoff, 2008). These booms were generally stimulated by rising credit leading to sharp increases in household leverage.

Credit booms can be instigated by a number of factors, for instance, shocks such as positive productivity shocks, economic policies and capital flows. As in the majority of earlier crises, the rapid expansion of credit also played an instrumental role in the run-up to the GFC. Credit aggregates rose quickly in Iceland, Ireland, Spain, the U.K., and several eastern European countries, often fueling real estate booms. Although aggregate credit growth was less pronounced, demonstrating slower corporate credit expansion, household indebtedness in the U.S. which surged after 2000, propelled increased mortgage financing, coupled with contributions from historically low interest rates and financial innovation. Despite low interest rates, debt service relative to disposable income reached record highs.

The mechanisms linking credit booms to crises included an upsurge in the leverage of borrowers and lenders as well as a decline in lending standards. In the GFC, both channels were at work. Increased leverage, partly ascribed to insufficient oversight, left households susceptible to a decline in house prices, a tightening in credit conditions, and a slowdown in economic activity. Not only did the correction hurt consumers as they ran into debt-servicing difficulties, it also resulted in systemic risks. And default rates were higher where credit growth had been more rapid.

Again, credit booms are generally linked to a worsening in lending standards. They often imply the creation of marginal assets that are feasible only as long as favorable economic conditions prevail. In the U.S. and elsewhere, a significant proportion of the mortgage expansion comprised of loans provided to borrowers with limited credit and employment histories, and often on terms poorly fitting to the borrowers' conditions. Debt servicing and repayment were susceptible to economic downturns and changes in credit and monetary conditions. This situation maximized default correlations across loans, creating portfolios exposed to declines in housing prices.

In other countries, the same pattern denoted large portions of credit denominated in foreign currency. Similar exposures had been prevalent before, for instance, prior to the East Asian financial crisis of 1997 in the corporate and financial sectors. In the GFC, large portions of credit in many Eastern European economies were denominated in foreign currency. Although interest rates lower than those on local currency loans increased affordability, borrowers' ability to service those loans was based on continued exchange rate stability. This implied high default risk correlations across loans and systemic exposure to macroeconomic shocks.

Risky liability structure in financial intermediaries typically heightens vulnerabilities. The significance of wholesale bank funding, which in the past often was in the form of foreign liabilities, especially in emerging market crises, exhibited itself this time in the nonbank financial system, especially in the U.S. Furthermore, commercial banks and investment banks in many advanced economies raised their leverage sharply. Due to buoyant housing and corporate financing markets, favorable conditions stimulated the emergence of large-scale derivatives markets, such as those for mortgage-backed securities and collateralized debt obligations with payoffs that relied on underlying asset prices.

Crises often are a result of expansions instigated by poorly sequenced regulatory reforms and financial liberalization. Improperly developed domestic financial systems have often been unable to intermediate large capital inflows in the wake of capital account liberalization. Weaknesses in supervision often resulted in currency and maturity mismatches and to large and concentrated credit risks. In the GFC also, regulatory approaches and prudential oversight were insufficient to limit excessive risk taking.

As in the past crises, financial institutions, merchant banks, investment banks, and off-balance-sheet vehicles of commercial banks functioned outside the regulatory perimeter. The shadow banking system was able to develop without much oversight, ultimately turning into a systemic risk. Derivatives markets were primarily unregulated and poorly supervised, building up the potential for chain reactions leading to systemic risk. The activities of financial institutions were not effectively monitored. Market discipline was not successful in preventing the buildup of systemic risks.

Similar to previous crises, prevention and early intervention mechanisms were also not adequate. Prior to the crisis, authorities gave top priority mainly to the liquidity and solvency of individual institutions, rather than to the resilience of the overall financial system. This lapse brought about an underestimation of the probability and costs of systemic risk. Moreover, as was prevalent in earlier episodes, intervention came late in many countries, substantially increasing the real and fiscal costs, and hindering the post-crisis recovery. At the global level, lack of proper coordination between the regulators and supervisors and the paucity of clear procedures for the resolution of global financial institutions obstructed efforts to prevent the cross-border transmission of the crisis.

4.4 New Factors

The GFC disclosed some new factors in terms of its origins and gravity. They included: (a) extensive implementation of complex and nontransparent financial instruments; (b) the high level of interconnectedness of financial market and financial institutions; (c) the high degree of leverage of financial institutions; and (d) the key role of the household sector.

First of all, the progressive expansion of complex securities and the growing delinking between borrowers and lenders exacerbated agency problems. Risks assignments became vague and incentives for due diligence worsened, resulting in inadequate monitoring by loan originators and an emphasis on boosting volumes to generate fees. The weaknesses in the rating process resulted in inflated and less informative risk ratings and masked the degree of risk exposure in some institutions.

Secondly, financial integration had increased considerably, particularly among advanced countries. Capital account openness and financial market reforms brought about vast increases in cross-border gross positions. There was also a growing presence of foreign intermediaries in a host of banking systems. Consequently, international risk sharing, competition and efficiency soared together with the risk of transmitting financial shocks across borders.

Increasing interconnectedness of financial institutions and markets and highly correlated financial risks deepened cross-border spillovers through many channels. Emerging markets—particularly those who relied heavily on external financing, and paradoxically those with more liquid markets—were impacted through capital account and bank funding pressures.

The sheer size of the U.S. financial market and its central role as investment destination also played some part to the spreading of the crisis. Any shock to the U.S. financial markets and economy was bound to have global impacts as U.S. financial assets represented about 31 percent of global financial assets and the U.S. dollar share in reserve currency was about 62 percent (Claessens *et al.*, 2010).

The third factor was the build-up of an exceptionally high degree of leverage of financial institutions and borrowers that was also responsible for the transmission of shocks. Leverage rose sharply in the financial sector, directly at commercial banks in Europe, and through the shadow banking system and the rising share of investment banks and non-deposit-taking institutions in the U.S. Moreover, the high leverage restricted the system's ability to absorb even small losses and contributed to the rapid fall in confidence and rise in counterparty risk early on in the crisis.

As financial institutions encountered heavy losses and wrote down illiquid securities, solvency concerns across markets stimulated a process of rapid deleveraging and forced asset sales. Hedge funds—facing financing constraints and redemption pressures—further fueled this rapid unwinding process which resulted in further asset price declines, inspiring distressed asset sales, rising recapitalization needs, and leading to a further loss of confidence.

The build-up in leverage was not limited to advanced countries. In some emerging economies, vulnerabilities pertaining to rising dependence on external financing flows increased. Many emerging economies unexpectedly found foreign funding sources very scarce and were threatened with sudden stops or reversals of capital flows.

The last factor was the difficulties in the household sector; in contrast, whereas most previous episodes of financial distress emanated from troubles in the official sector (for instance, Latin America's debt crisis of the early 1980s) or the corporate sector (for instance, the East Asian financial crisis), it was the difficulties in the household sector that played a crucial part in this crisis. The origins of the GFC, however, had largely to do with the overextended households, especially *via* non-traditional mortgage loans and especially in the U.S. This high household leverage had implications for how the crisis was being transferred from the financial to the real sector and complicated the resolution mechanisms and policy responses. The overextension of the household sector turned into risky assets whose value depended directly or indirectly on ever soaring house prices. So, when the financial turmoil ensued, households were not properly positioned to absorb losses.

In the U.S., a vicious cycle of growing foreclosures, falling home values and disappearing securitization markets developed rapidly. An upsurge of finance company failures—no longer able to securitize subprime mortgages—resulted in a near breakdown in mortgage origination and more abrupt adjustment.

Household balance sheet vulnerabilities also grew in other advanced countries and in many emerging markets. As real estate prices plummeted, this had an adverse impact on the quality of loan portfolios and put financial intermediaries at risk.

4.5 Policy Responses

Policy responses undertaken during the course of the GFC can be categorized under three headings: improving the macroeconomic situation, encouraging market stability, and advancing structural repair (Truman, 2009).

In terms of improving the macroeconomic environment, beginning in the summer of 2007, the monetary authorities generally acted rather swiftly to implement measures responding to the demand by financial institutions for much greater access to central bank liquidity. Central banks loosened the terms of access to discount windows and utilized an array of similar tools and these actions were well coordinated. Coordination between the major central banks was strengthened in December 2007 with the setting up of Federal Reserve swap facilities.

The use of conventional monetary policy and reductions in interest rate took place later for some countries.[2] Sometimes, monetary policy actions were coordinated, but this was common only during the second year of the crisis. As part of the containment phase of the crisis, some central banks adopted the so-called unconventional monetary policies with respect to what they purchase, on what terms, and whether they are concerned about the consequences for the liability sides of their balance sheets.

It was only during the second year of the crisis, starting in late 2008, that discretionary fiscal policy came to be extensively employed by those countries with room to do so and such policy also provided a substantial stimulus. Many countries, including the U.S., U.K., Germany and China declared major packages to support demand in 2009 and 2010. In aggregate, discretionary fiscal measures announced since late 2008 provided for a stimulus of up to 2 percent of world GDP in 2009, as governments moved forward to fill part of the contraction in private spending (Edey, 2009). This support took the form of direct financial assistance to households, tax reductions for businesses and direct spending by governments. This was in addition to the impacts of the automatic fiscal stabilizers—such as the typical reduction in the level of taxes paid by the private sector during downturns and the increase in unemployment benefit spending—which in some countries have also been quite significant.

With respect to measures for promoting financial market stability, these measures often combine into monetary policy actions, and contribute to structural repair as well as to market stability. However, this type of measures is unique in the sense that it is directed mainly at actual or observed market failures rather than at institutions, individually or as a group. Normally, these measures utilize the central bank's balance sheet. The general aim is to provide liquidity to particular markets, for instance the commercial paper market, and thus to reestablish their functioning as suppliers of credit. One measure of this kind that does not relate to central banks is raising the coverage of deposit insurance, which is designed to stabilize the market for bank deposits.

The U.S. progressed further in this direction than most other countries owing to two factors. Firstly, nonbank financial institutions formed a larger part of the overall financial system in the U.S. than in other countries. Thus, direct market-related measures were required to restore the flow of credit. Secondly, the Federal Reserve had the power to act under unusual and urgent circumstances to use its balance sheet to facilitate this kind of action. Hence, it was much easier within the U.S. political system to approach the central bank, where the money is, than in some other countries.

The group of policy measures pertaining to advancing structural repair appear to be quite controversial. At least five types of action with progressive levels of intrusion in the functioning of financial institutions were employed. The first included guarantees of the liabilities (other than deposits) of certain types of financial institutions, generally banks but, for example in the U.S., money market mutual funds also whose use has been rife. The second included capital injections that were utilized in a number of countries, but with different restrictions attached based on the jurisdiction and the circumstances of the institutions. The third kind of action refer to programs concerning legacy, or toxic assets by moving those assets off of the balance sheets of institutions. A fourth type was the takeover of a financial institution (or of group of institutions) either *de jure* or through a process that did not involve formal nationalization but implied considerable governmental control. The last one referred to institutions that were forced into mergers or into bankruptcy. Though these two events are different in many aspects, they have one common structural feature: the institution vanishes.

4.6 Impact on Developing Economies

The GFC affected both financial systems across the globe and economic activity in almost all countries, including the developing countries. Even those countries that had bolstered their policies and built defenses to resist a less benign global environment than that which existed for much of the previous decade were not spared.

In 2003-07, the developing world witnessed an impressive economic boom, rising at a rate of 7 percent per year. The boom was driven by a combination of three elements prevailing in the global markets including exceptional financing, high commodity prices and, for many countries, large flows of remittances. The economic and financial crisis, however, was propelled by the reversal of these three positive elements that developing countries witnessed during the boom period (Griffith-Jones and Ocampo, 2009). The first trigger that led to the reversals of these trends was the effect of the bursting of the U.S. housing bubble. However, it was the reversal in commodity prices in mid-2008 and, especially, the global financial crisis that began in September 2008 that resulted in the reversal of favorable global conditions for developing countries. The recession in the U.S. and other developed countries further aggravated the adverse effects of the crisis for developing countries.

A year after the crisis erupted, commodity prices continued to boom. This, coupled with high foreign exchange reserves, helped to attract capital to the developing countries even after the outburst of the subprime crisis. However, both joined the downturn later on.

The crisis was transmitted to the developing world from the U.S. and Europe through various means. Balance sheets had not been exposed to the toxic assets that dominated positions in the major institutions. Derivatives were employed less frequently and were generally limited to the more traditional instruments employed to hedge against currency and other risks linked to trade. Financial institutions in the EMEs either shied away from the more exotic tools such as credit default swaps and collateralized debt obligations or were prevented by regulation from holding or trading such instruments (Boorman, 2009). Ultimately, this did not protect these countries.

The developing economies were affected through a number of channels. In the first place, there was the withdrawal of funds by some major financial institutions from their subsidiaries based in these economies. The contraction of the balance sheets of some major institutions and the need to rebuild their capital base restricted the funding available to other institutions in both the industrial countries (for instance, hedge funds) and in the emerging world that depended on dollar (or even euro) funding.

The second channel was the seizing-up of the international credit markets. Credit flows through the international banks and global bond markets to developing countries dried up. This generated considerable financial stress in some of those countries that had very large current account deficits and took on substantial international debt.

In aggregate, developing economies—especially those that were too much indebted and encountered huge financing requirements both from current account deficit as well as from the need to refinance maturing debt—witnessed a sharp decline in all the major categories of capital inflows. Some of the worst affected countries also experienced massive capital flight and significant depreciations of their currencies. This was all reflected in a sharp drop in international reserves, with almost all of the developing economies in all regions of the world other than East Asia registering significant declines.

Thirdly, there was the impact of the crisis on economic activity—in the first instance, in the U.S. and Europe, and later in Japan. Initially, this was exhibited in a sharp contraction in exports from those developing countries that had become the top exporters to the industrial world. Quite rapidly, however, exports declined from the other developing economies, that is, those whose exports comprised of raw and intermediate goods shipped to those larger economies, especially China.

This drop in exports produced an internal feedback loop wherein the initial reduction in trade weakened the domestic economies of the developing countries, with further negative feedback on the financial sectors in those countries as the quality of domestic credit deteriorated.

Another channel through which the developing countries were affected was through remittances, an important source of income and foreign exchange. While total remittances to developing countries was US$ 278 billion in 2007 and increased to US$ 325 billion in 2008, it fell to US$ 308 billion in 2009 (Mohapatra *et al.*, 2011).

An important avenue of foreign currency earnings in many developing countries was tourism. Since September 2008 the number of air passengers in the world dropped sharply. Although a good part of this drop was ascribed to reduced travel for business purposes, it also included less tourist travel, as households reduced consumption on luxury goods, and secondly, mortgages for overseas holidays were becoming harder to procure (Naude, 2009).

Likewise, private investment flows to developing countries declined as more risk averse investors moved their funds to perceived 'safer' havens. This included both portfolio flows and FDI. Reduced portfolio flows also affected government borrowing. The costs of sovereign bonds and commercial debt—both important sources of finance for developing-country governments—rose sharply. On the other hand, FDI to developing countries responded very little with respect to the crisis, in contrast to other flows, with a peak of US$ 574 billion in 2007, a slight increase to US$ 650 billion in 2008 and a sharp decline to US$ 519 billion in 2009 (UNCTAD, 2012).

The combination of banking failures and decreases in domestic lending, decreases in export earnings, and decreases in financial flows to developing countries ended up lowering private sector investments and household consumption to some extent. This subsequently led to reduced government expenditure, as governments faced the higher cost of raising funds along with less tax income.

The general impact of the GFC on developing countries was negative. Some countries were more negatively affected, particularly those reliant on trade with the United States, those with balance-of-payments problems and large fiscal deficits, and those with inappropriately regulated financial sectors. In essence, the crisis exposed countries with poor macroeconomic management and weak financial institutions. Still, a number of large developing countries could go away with the crisis in a short period of time due to a number of factors. First of all, the epicenter of the crisis was in the developed countries. The crisis came about as an exogenous shock and not due to inappropriate domestic policies, as in the earlier episodes. Secondly, developing-country banks were not directly impacted as most of the banks were marginally exposed to the U.S. subprime crisis. Third, many developing-country economies were much more resilient due to satisfactory growth, better policies, and having learned lessons during the East Asian financial crisis. For instance, after the East Asian financial crisis, the affected countries in the region adopted the Economic Review and Policy Dialogue, the Chiang Mai Agreement, and the Asian Bond Markets Initiative, all of which contributed to financial development and stabilization in the region (Kuroda, 2008).

The policy responses to the GFC have varied among the affected developing countries. Because of the impact of the crisis on the availability of capital through the global financial markets, many countries entered into swap arrangements in order to strengthen their reserve positions. The greatest of such operations was the U.S. Federal Reserve System entering into temporary reciprocal currency arrangements for the provision of dollar liquidity with Brazil, Mexico, Singapore and Republic of Korea. Other bilateral swap arrangements were agreed or increased. A large number of developing economies also approached the IMF for support.

Some countries took steps to address the impact on the banking sector and the financial sector more generally of both the direct effects of the financial crisis and the evolving effect of dwindling domestic economies. In developing economies, deposit insurance schemes were modified to broaden the kinds of deposits encompassed or to raise the maximum amount covered. A group of countries in Asia that did not have deposit insurance schemes previously introduced them as a technique of encouraging public confidence in their banking systems. Other steps targeted at the banking and financial systems included capital injections and other support mechanisms for domestic banks, both to assist banks in meeting minimum capital adequacy standards and to support bank lending operations, particularly in the critical area of trade credit. Many of the measures were *ad hoc* and faced the same problem that surfaced in the more advanced countries, that is, the consistency and coordination across borders of measures to strengthen the domestic banking systems.

Along with most of the world's more advanced economies, a large number of EMEs also announced ambitious fiscal stimulus packages. For instance, the EMEs that were members of the G20 took drastic steps to bolster domestic activity. Still, there was significant disparity across the EMEs with respect to the composition of these stimulus packages. About one-third of the measures, on average, constituted of direct government tax cuts and other revenue measures to encourage private spending, and about two-thirds formed expenditure measures. In almost all the countries the expenditure measures were largely weighted towards infrastructure spending. For instance, in China, the stimulus package consisted only of expenditure measures whereas in India, about one-third of the measures were temporary indirect tax reductions.

Immediate and short-term policy responses were needed to ensure that (i) the impact of the financial crisis was minimized; (ii) confidence in financial systems was revived; and (iii) that the impact on the real economy was curtailed. Over the longer term, countries needed to focus on strengthening their financial systems within the purview of reforming the global financial architecture (Naude, 2009). A glimpse of the responses including the immediate, short-term and long-term measures to tackle the adverse effects of the crisis is presented in Appendix 4.2.

4.7 Impact on Least Developed Countries

The initial impact of GFC on the least developed countries (LDCs) was less pronounced because of their less integration with the world financial markets. With the deepening of the financial crisis, freezing of credit, and the plunge in the market value of private wealth, the financial crisis converted into a crisis of the real economy beginning in the fall of 2008. It was then that the LDCs were affected more during this phase of real economic crisis (Karshenas, 2009).

One of the principal mechanisms through which the LDCs were impacted was through a sharp reduction in world trade and rapid decline in commodity prices. Prior to the crisis, the share of LDC trade in the world markets had been steadily taking an upward trend. Owing to the increases in the prices of oil and minerals as well as the preferential market access in the developing country markets, the share of LDCs in world merchandise trade in 2008 accounted for 1.1 percent, up from 0.6 percent in 2000 (WTO; 2009). However, as the major developed countries such as the U.S. and the EU began witnessing a decline in their aggregate demand, exports from the LDCs also fell. According to ITC (2010), exports by LDCs to major partners plummeted by 34 percent in 2009.

Another channel through which the LDCs were affected was through FDI flows. Inflows of FDI to LDCs declined in 2009 and 2010. In 2010, FDI in the amount of US$ 26 billion was around US$ 6 billion less than in 2008, when it accounted for $32 billion (UNCTAD, 2011). Interestingly, net flows of FDI were also not severely affected by the GFC as LDCs showed resilience during the peak of the crisis (Audiguier, 2012).

A third transmission mechanism, which was of significance for some LDCs, was the slowdown in remittance flows. As unemployment in the advanced countries increased and the end of the commodity export boom in some of the labor importing developing countries curtailed the demand for migrant labor, the growth rate of remittances slowed down, but nevertheless continued to be positive, reaching 5.7 percent in 2009 and 6.8 percent in 2010.

The economic crisis also led to a sharp deterioration in the fiscal position of all advanced economies as these countries utilized resources to provide stimulus to their own economies and continued to bailout the financial institutions that were at the center of the crisis (Bhattacharya and Dasgupta, 2012). There was also pressure on the Official Development Assistance (ODA) budget of the Organization for Economic Cooperation and Development (OECD) countries that had adverse consequences for the LDCs. Since most LDCs continued to be highly indebted, the prospect of reduced aid flows put pressure on LDC governments to maintain a balance between investing for development and paying back loans, leading to less resources being allocated to development needs.

Overall, the effect of the GFC on the LDCs was multifaceted. It impacted different countries in different ways, based on the mode of integration of the particular LDC in the global economy and the structure of its domestic economy as well as the policy response by the LDC governments.

In terms of the responses to the GFC by the LDCs, a number of LDC governments were able to sustain public spending in 2009, some of them with massive support from multilateral donors. However, with limited fiscal space, only some LDCs were able to implement discretionary countercyclical interventions. Moreover, Asian LDCs were more proactive than other LDCs, taking advantage of the larger financial resources at their disposal, and preferring spending over tax measures.[3]

With regard to monetary policy, several LDCs where inflation had drastically fallen in the wake of the crisis adopted moderately accommodating monetary policies to foster a faster recovery. While monetary expansion was, to some extent, helpful, it had only a limited impact in LDCs owing to their low degree of financial development and the small size of their secondary bond markets.

In 2009, many LDCs with floating (or managed-floating) exchange rate regimes permitted their nominal exchange rates to depreciate against major currencies to facilitate an adjustment of their current accounts and sustain the tradable sector. This was especially true in the case of a few large commodity exporters such as the Democratic Republic of the Congo and Zambia. On the other spectrum, LDCs that could use their stock of reserves accumulated before the crisis, such as Bangladesh, Cambodia and the United Republic of Tanzania, chose maintaining a fairly stable exchange rate *vis-à-vis* the dollar (UNCTAD, 2010).

To minimize the impact of the crisis on the LDCs, specific policies were required at the global level. This was acknowledged by the international community as testified by action plans by international financial institutions such as the IMF and the World Bank as well as the references made to the predicament of the low income countries in the Global Plan for Recovery and Reform by G20 in its London meeting in April 2009. The G20 agreement comprised a US$ 1.1 trillion program of support to restore credit in the global economy. Especially, the resources available to IMF was to be trebled to US$ 750 billion, and SDR allocations were to be raised by US$ 250 billion.

The G20 communiqué recognized the disproportionate impact of the crisis on the vulnerable groups in the LDCs and its potential long durable effect on the global economy. It reaffirmed the commitment and the need to fulfil the ODA pledges, including debt relief and the Gleneagles commitments to achieve these goals. The plan stipulated that US$ 50 billion of the total additional resources committed to combat the global crisis would be allocated for the low income countries, and a further US$ 6 billion to be pledged from the sale of IMF gold to provide concessional funding to the LDCs over the next two to three years (Karshenas, 2009).

Overall, LDCs demonstrated growth resilience and their average growth rate remained high by historical standards.

What differs from past crises was that output declines across LDCs and other countries were unusually synchronized. LDCs, less open and less financially integrated in the global economy, were thus less affected than expected due to the nature of the crisis by itself. Moreover, they benefited from higher growth rates from 2000 to 2007 and then entered the crisis with a better economic situation than in the past (Audiguier, 2012).

4.8 Lessons Drawn

A prime factor responsible for the GFC was inadequate and ineffective regulation and supervision both within and across those countries that hosted the global financial centers and the major international financial institutions. The GFC demonstrated that there were some shortcomings in the prevailing policy considerations in several aspects. These included the following:

1. Market discipline together with poor prudential regulation was ineffective in limiting risk-taking outside the banking sector (IMF, 2009).[4]
2. The systemic importance of some nonbanks was underappreciated, including their potential effect on major financial markets and confidence.[5]
3. Regulation did not properly consider the systemic risks posed by the interaction between regulated and unregulated institutions, activities and markets.[6]
4. Investors depended too much on credit ratings, which primarily focused on default risks, and subject to growing conflicts of interest in rating structured products.
5. The GFC provided a clear example of major gaps in information, including some large risk exposures, both on- and off-balance sheet, that were unappreciated or unreported and the pricing and scheme of complex structured credit products that were unclear to many investors.
6. The crisis also illustrated limitations in the early warning frameworks used to gauge systemic and institutional risks.[7]

A number of lessons can be drawn from the GFC. One, the crisis provided lessons for redesigning central bank liquidity framework to facilitate more effective crisis management in the future. In crises and periods of market dysfunctionality, it was no longer appropriate to target a single short-term market rate, and central banks had to take into account a broader range of short-term rates and their effect on term rates and the macro-economy. Moreover, there is a need of caution to make sure that changes in operational frameworks offset the need for a firm response despite systemic shocks against the risk of moral hazard, especially when the emergency measures have been put in place for an extended period.

Two, the crisis demonstrated the critical need for better mechanisms for providing cross border liquidity including permanent arrangements for cross-border liquidity provision. Major central banks—especially the U.S. Federal Reserve—set up swap lines that have tackled cross-currency pressures (IMF, 2009).

Three, it was learnt from the GFC that the potential scope of regulation and supervision has to be widened in order to ensure that all financial activities that pose systemic risks are adequately captured. Investors and authorities must be able to better evaluate and limit the build-up of systemic risk and address the tendency for activity to shift to unregulated or off-balance sheet entities (Claessens *et al.*, 2010). This calls for a broader perimeter of regulation, particularly when institutions become systemically relevant, to enable corrective measures.

Four, supervisory oversight of liquidity management practices should be accorded equal attention as that of solvency risk. Adherence to sound liquidity management principles should be given equal attention by supervisors and markets, as exposures to credit and market risk.

Five, there is a need to improve financial institutions' failure resolution frameworks. To lower moral hazard emanating from public support expectations and the risks of disorderly collapse, regulatory authorities should have the power to shut down or restructure troubled financial institutions—both banks and nonbanks—outside standard bankruptcy processes. This demands robust legal processes for early intervention and resolution of weak financial institutions, compatible across legal jurisdictions.

Six, regulations need to provide incentives to firms to smooth the impact of macroeconomic shocks. Countercyclical capital regulation and loan loss provisioning requirements should be vital constituents of such a framework. This could take the shape of altering liquidity, collateral, capital, or loan loss provisioning requirements when asset prices, loan growth, or leverage deviate significantly from their long-run trends.

Seven, the limited effectiveness of and potential distortions related to unilateral policies in a financial integrated world underscore the need for policy coordination. Cooperation will be increasingly vital as financial systems become more integrated. Coordination among host- and home-country regulators and monetary authorities will also be important when it comes to liquidity (and solvency) support in case of a bust.

Eight, market discipline has not been very effective in complementing supervision. Improvement demands enhanced disclosure of information on off-balance sheet commitments, firms' liquidity profiles, and risk exposures and concentrations both within and between financial institutions.

Nine, the crisis has illustrated the significance of central banks in enhancing financial stability through timely emergency liquidity provision and, at times, peculiar market operations. Supervisors and central banks need to cooperate with each other to obtain and share information necessary for the conduct of monitoring systemic risk (Farrar *et al.*, 2009). Central banks need to have access to all essential information in order to assess systemic risks to the macro-economy and the payments system, as well as evaluate counterparty risks for monetary and emergency liquidity operations.

Ten, agencies involved in regulation, supervision, and crisis management should have clear mandates and instruments commensurate with these mandates, particularly in safeguarding financial stability. At the national level, the organization of supervision can be improved by developing a clear distribution of responsibilities among the relevant agencies. Consistent supervision demands ample resources, close communication, and a flow of information among all parties responsible for oversight and financial crisis management, including central banks and finance ministries.

Eleven, global coordination is a necessary condition for managing a global crisis. From that perspective, the G20 Summit held in London in April 2009 was a clear turning point when the leaders of the world displayed extraordinary determination and unity. The entire gamut of crisis response measures—accommodative monetary stance, fiscal stimulus, debt and deposit guarantees, capital injection, asset purchases, currency swaps—were drawn in varying ways from the G20 package.

Twelve, one major lesson was that price stability and macroeconomic stability do not guarantee financial stability. The years before the crisis were characterized by steady growth and low and stable inflation in advanced economies and rapid growth and development in EMEs. There was a growing consensus that the best practice in monetary policy framework is the pursuit of a single target (price stability) by means of a single instrument (short-term policy interest rate). As the global financial sector came to the verge of a collapse even in the midst of a period of extraordinary price stability, it became evident that price stability does not necessarily guarantee financial stability.

Finally, microprudential regulation and supervision has to be supplemented by macroprudential oversight. The crisis had shown that a group of healthy financial institutions does not necessarily make a healthy financial sector since there are complex interconnections in the financial sector across banks, other financial institutions, and markets, and a problem in any part of the system can quickly transmit through the system and grow into a crisis.

Appendix 4.1: Global Financial Crisis: Chronology of Important Events

2007	Events
2 April	The first signs of trouble in the U.S. housing market are witnessed as subprime specialist lender New Century Financial files for bankruptcy.
31 July	Investment bank Bear Stearns liquidates two hedge funds that invested in risky securities backed by subprime mortgage loans.
6 Aug.	American Home Mortgage Investment, which specializes in adjustable-rate mortgages, files for bankruptcy protection.
9 Aug.	French bank BNP Paribas suspends three funds that invested in the U.S. mortgage market.
16 Aug.	Fitch Ratings slashes the credit rating of giant mortgage lender Countrywide Financial to its third-lowest investment-grade rating.
12 Dec.	The Federal Reserve introduces the Term Auction Facility to supply short-term credit to banks with subprime mortgages.
2008	
11 Jan.	Bank of America, the biggest U.S. bank by market value, agrees to buy Countrywide Financial for about $4 billion.
13 Feb.	The Economic Stimulus Act of 2008 is enacted, which includes a tax rebate.
16 Mar.	JP Morgan agrees to buy Bear Stearns, which is on the brink of collapse due to its exposure to the failing subprime investments.
24 Mar.	New York Fed provides $29 billion in term financing to assist JP Morgan in purchasing Bear Stearns.
11 July	Federal regulators seize IndyMac Federal Bank after it becomes the largest regulated thrift to fail.
30 July	The Housing and Economic Recovery Act of 2008 is enacted.

7 Sep.	Mortgage giants Fannie Mae and Freddie Mac are taken over by the government.
15 Sep.	Bank of America agrees to purchase Merrill Lynch for $50 billion. Lehman Brothers files for bankruptcy-court protection.
16 Sep.	American International Group, the world's largest insurer, accepts a $85 billion federal bailout that provides the government a 79.9% stake in the company.
21 Sep.	Goldman Sachs and Morgan Stanley, the last two independent investment banks, will become bank holding companies subject to greater regulation by the Federal Reserve.
25 Sep.	Federal regulators shut down Washington Mutual Bank and its branches and assets are sold to JPMorgan Chase in the biggest U.S. bank failure in history.
29 Sep.	Congress rejects a $700 billion Wall Street financial rescue package, known as the Troubled Asset Relief Program (TARP), sending the Dow Jones industrial average down 778 points, its single-worst point drop ever.
3 Oct.	Wells Fargo & Co., the biggest U.S. bank on the West Coast, agrees to buy Wachovia for about $14.8 billion. Congress passes the Emergency Economic Stabilization Act of 2008.
28 Oct.	The Treasury buys $125 billion worth of preferred stock of nine banks in first TARP funding wave.
10 Nov.	The Treasury buys $40 billion of AIG shares through TARP.
25 Nov.	The Term Asset-Backed Securities Loan Facility is announced.
16 Dec.	The federal funds rate is lowered to zero percent.
19 Dec.	On 19 December 2008, President Bush agreed to a US$ 24.9 bailout using TARP: $13.4 billion for General Motors, US$ 5.5 billion for Chrysler, and US$ 5 billion for General Motors Acceptance Corp.

2009	
16 Jan.	The Treasury announces it will lend $1.5 billion in TARP funds to Chrysler to extend new consumer auto loans.
13 Feb.	Congress approves the American Recovery and Reinvestment Act of 2009, a $787 billion economic stimulus package.
25 Feb.	The Federal Reserve, FDIC and other government offices announce plan to 'stress test' banks by April 2009.
6 Mar.	The Dow Jones hit its lowest level of 6,443.27 point.
7 May	Regulators release results of stress tests on 19 biggest U.S. banks, all of which obtained TARP funds, and say 10 of them need to raise a combined $74.6 billion to withstand a possibly deeper recession.
1 June	General Motors and three domestic subsidiaries announce they have filed to reorganize in bankruptcy.
1 Nov.	CIT Group Inc. files for bankruptcy protection under Chapter 11, wiping out the $2.3 billion stake the government bought in CIT through TARP in December 2008.
2 Dec.	Bank of America says it will buy back all the stock it sold to the Treasury and TARP.
14 Dec.	Citigroup and Wells Fargo make similar announcements.

Source: *USA Today*, 8 September 2013; Wikipedia, "Financial Crisis of 2007-2008".

Appendix 4.2: Summary of Responses to Global Financial Crisis by Developing Countries

Timeframe	Objective	Policy options
Immediate	Containment of financial panic	Guarantee bank deposits Guarantee inter bank loans Provide liquidity to banks Forbearance on regulations
Short term	Resolution measures	Recapitalize banks Mergers and acquisition in financial sector
	Monetary expansion	Reductions in the costs of borrowing Raise inflation targets
	Fiscal expansion	Increase in spending on social safety nets, including conditional and unconditional grants and public works
	Trade expansion	Lowering of protective measures Maintain competitive exchange rates
Long term	Domestic financial development	Increase the access to finance Improve domestic resource mobilization Improve efficiency of banking sector Avoid financial repression Improve supervision and regulation Strengthen property and contract rights, judiciary and rule of law Proceed, but with caution, with financial openness
	Reform of international financial architecture	Move to a more inclusive system of global financial governance Improve the share, efficiency and management of global aid system Reform Bretton Woods Institutions

Source: Naude (2009).

NOTES

1. A list of the major events during the GFC is presented in Appendix 4.1.
2. Interest rates in advanced and emerging-market countries were slashed sharply as the crisis evolved. In a few advanced economies, policy rates were lowered to close to zero and central banks shifted to quantitative easing approaches to provide additional stimulus to specific markets and to the economy more generally. The pass-through of these decreases in policy rates to reduce private household and business sector rates was larger in some countries than in others (Edey, 2009).
3. For example, Bangladesh enacted three distinct stimulus packages during the crisis, allocating resources primarily to the agricultural sector, to the extension of safety-net program and to the support of SMEs and the apparel industry. Likewise, Cambodia permitted its target budget deficit for 2009 to increase to over 4 percent of GDP, combining both spending measures and tax breaks for the garment industry and the agricultural sector (UNCTAD, 2010).
4. Some unregulated companies, for instance, were able to assume both credit risks and substantial liquidity risks, funding poor quality long-term securities by short-term borrowings with high degrees of leverage.
5. For instance, the failure of Lehman Brothers and the insolvency event of two Bear Stearns managed hedge funds seemed to have an astonishingly large effects (IMF, 2009).
6. Bank regulation, for instance, did not fully signal risks from off-balance sheet vehicles or loan originators with poor underwriting standards.
7. For instance, standard financial soundness indicators (FSIs), though beneficial in their own right, may not be enough as leading indicators of vulnerability. Commonly used FSIs, such as capital adequacy ratios (CARs) relied on the underlying assessment of asset quality, and in the run up to the GFC, understated the risks linked to complex structured products on banks' trading books and off-balance sheet transactions.

Chapter 5

Selected Financial Crises

5.1 Introduction

Until the 1930s, both financial crises and debt cycles were recognized with respect to cycles of classic capitalism. From the 1960s, however, economics, to some extent, overlooked the contributions of this important analytical and empirical tradition. At the same time, most economists were not interested in the historical perspective with regard to finance, and many contended that the old business cycles had come to an end after the Bretton Woods (Marichal, 2009). The outburst of the Latin American debt crises in the 1980s compelled a number of researchers to focus their interest on international finance and some to look again to banking and monetary history to scrutinize past crises, especially the Great Depression. However, this interest in explaining financial trends in the long run was surpassed in the 1990s by the fascination with global finance.

Against this background, this chapter will undertake a review of some of the crises in the past and provide some lessons. These crises include the Stock Market Crash of 1929 along with the Great Depression of the 1930s, the international debt crisis of the 1980s, Russia's financial crisis of 1998, Turkey's financial crisis of 2001, Argentina's financial crisis of 2001, and European debt crisis of 2010.

5.2 Stock Market Crash of 1929 and the Great Depression

The Stock Market Crash of 1929 began on 24 October 1929, with wary investors trading a record 12.9 million shares. On 28 October, the Dow Jones Industrial Average plunged nearly 13 percent. The market plummeted another 12 percent the next day. While the crisis conveyed shock waves across the financial world, there were many signs that a stock market crash was imminent.

While the exact reason of the Crash of 1929 is often debated among economists, there are some widely accepted theories. Some experts argue that at the time of the crash, stocks were exorbitantly overpriced and that a collapse was imminent. That same kind of overconfidence extended to average consumers and small investors, too, resulting in an "asset bubble." The crash took place after a long period of increasing market growth that led to consumer overconfidence. As a matter of fact, after 1922, the stock market had soared by almost 20 percent each year until 1929 (Marks, 2018).

Again, during the 1920s, there was a rapid expansion in bank credit and easily acquired loans. People were not scared of debt due to the market's stability. The concept of 'buying on margin' gave opportunities for people with little financial insight to borrow money from their stockbroker and put down as little as 10 percent of the share value.

An analogous kind of overconfidence was witnessed in industries such as manufacturing and agriculture: there was an overproduction of items including farm crops, steel, durable goods and iron, implying that companies had to clear their supplies at a loss as a result of which the share prices suffered.

Moreover, in August 1929—a few weeks prior to the crash of the stock market—the Federal Reserve Bank of New York hiked the interest rate from 5 percent to 6 percent. This steep, sudden rise cooled investor enthusiasm, which impacted market stability and lowered economic growth. Another cause was an ongoing agricultural recession as farmers struggled to make an annual profit to keep their businesses afloat which impacted the financial climate of the country.

Another factor was the paucity of financial regulation in the years leading to the crash. Unregulated banks lent generously to speculators, who engorged the stock market to unsustainable levels. When it all came crashing down, there were no government protections for investors or the unemployed.

Public panic after the stock market collapse led to people running to banks to withdraw their funds in a number of 'bank runs', and investors were not able to return their money since bank officials had invested the money in the market. This resulted in enormous bank failures and further deepened an already dreadful financial situation.

One major lesson drawn was that strong and effective regulation is required for the financial system. The other lesson is the importance of diversification since during the course of the crash, stocks lost 40 percent of their value in one month and 90 percent in a period of three years. Likewise, it was also learnt that a number of apparent undramatic events may create a setting for a wide price decline. Thirdly, even a market that is not unduly high can burst. Hence, both market psychology and the underlying economics are important.

While historians sometimes debate whether Crash of 1929 was the main factor responsible for the Great Depression, there is no doubt that it impacted the American economy for many years. There are diverging opinions as to both the causes and consequences of the Great Depression. Many economists argued that the Crash in 1929 was poorly managed, among others, since the Federal Reserve did not increase the money supply sufficiently, and therefore constrained credit markets. In addition, the U.S. authorities persisted on rigidly sustaining the Gold Standard, which thus contributed to accentuating rigidities.

Early in 1928, while the U.S. possessed significant current account surplus, Germany's current account was in huge deficit. Borrowings by German public and private sector took place in foreign currencies *via* dollar denominated bonds and credits from the U.S., routed through banks in the Netherlands, Switzerland and Austria. Monetary contraction in the U.S. resulted in a depression in Germany. The Reichsbank's foreign reserves of gold and foreign exchange plummeted sharply.

In May 1931, the Kreditanstalt, Austria's largest bank, collapsed. As investors feared that their money would be frozen, there was a massive capital flight. Germany was not able to procure the foreign credits required to prevent the crisis from happening. To stop the capital outflow, Germany had to shut down banks, devalue the mark, negotiate standstill agreements with foreign creditors and impose exchange controls.

During the period 1930-32, money supply in the U.S. and Germany plummeted by 26 percent and 27 percent, respectively while it fell by 18 percent both in the United Kingdom and France.

The German currency and banking crisis affected the British pound. European banks whose assets were frozen by the German standstill agreements were undertaking massive withdrawals from the United Kingdom leading to a weakening of the pound. On 16 September 1931, United Kingdom suspended gold convertibility and permitted the pound to float.

By 1932, it was apparent that the U.S. and the world economy had already entered a Great Depression, and that massive financial reforms were required. Latin America was also hit hard. From 1931 onwards, most Latin American nations put an end to the Gold Standard, after the persistent efforts to remain faithful in the first two crisis years of 1929 and 1930. Many governments in the region also announced moratoriums on the servicing of foreign public debts at this time.[1]

By 1933, 35 countries had ended gold and gold-exchange standards. In 1932, as compared to the previous year, exports declined by 35 percent in France, 40 percent in Germany and 33 percent in the United States while it declined by 7 percent in the United Kingdom and 19 percent in Canada.

Economic recovery as enunciated by industrial activity was evident in the United Kingdom, France and Germany, with the U.S. experiencing an industrial upturn during April and May 1933. The "New Deal" of President Franklin Roosevelt produced a drastic reformation of the U.S. economy, setting the foundations of the American welfare state—federal aid to the unemployed, stiffer regulation of industry, legal protections for workers and the Social Security Program.

A number of lessons can be derived from the Great Depression. The first lesson is that a small fiscal expansion has only small impacts (Romer, 2009). Secondly, monetary expansion can assist in healing an economy even when interest rates are close to zero. A protracted period of monetary contraction will undermine time-dimension economic activity and wield adverse impacts on the economy (Gwartney *et al.*, 2010).

The third lesson that can be drawn is that financial recovery and real recovery go together. The fourth lesson is that tax cuts and upsurges in government spending can help restore a depressed economy, but only if they are used on a large scale.

5.3 International Debt Crisis

In the 1980s, the world witnessed a debt crisis in which highly indebted Latin American and other developing countries were unable to repay the debt. This was also known as a period of the 'lost decade.' This crisis involved long-term commercial bank debt which had ensued in the public sector (including debt owed by state-owned enterprises and guaranteed by the government).

The origin of the debt crisis can be traced back to the 1970s when two large oil price shocks created current account deficits in many Latin American countries. At the same time, these shocks created current account surpluses among oil-exporting countries. With the encouragement of the U.S. Government, large U.S. money-center banks were willing to act as intermediaries between the two groups, providing the exporting countries with a safe, liquid place for their funds and then lending those funds to Latin America.

Latin American borrowing from U.S. commercial banks and other creditors increased dramatically during the 1970s. At the end of 1970, total outstanding debt from all sources totaled only US$ 29 billion, but by the end of 1978, that number had skyrocketed to US$ 159 billion (FDIC, 1997). By 1982, the debt level reached US$ 327 billion.

Though the potential risk of the growing involvement of U.S. banks in Latin American and other developing countries' debt did not go unnoticed, still, by 1982, the nine largest U.S. money-center banks held Latin American debt amounting to 176 percent of their capital (Sachs, 1988).

The crisis was ultimately triggered in August 1982, when Mexico announced that it was unable to service its foreign debt which amounted to US$ 80 billion. Other countries followed suit. All in all, sixteen Latin American countries rescheduled their debts, as well as eleven developing countries in different parts of the globe (FDIC, 1997).

As the crisis swept beyond Mexico, the U.S. organized an "international lender of last resort," a joint rescue effort among commercial banks, central banks, and the IMF in August 1982. Under this program, commercial banks concurred to restructure the countries' debt, and the IMF and other official agencies lent the developing countries adequate funds to pay the interest, but not principal, on their loans. The developing countries, on the other hand, agreed to pursue structural reforms of their economies and to do away with the budget deficits.

Although this program averted an immediate crisis, it allowed the problem to aggravate. Instead of eliminating subsidies to state-owned enterprises, many countries slashed spending on infrastructure, health, and education, and froze wages or laid off state employees, leading to high unemployment, declines in per capita income, and stagnant or negative growth. (Carrasco, 1999).

After many years of negotiations with the debtor countries, it became evident that the majority of the loans would not be repaid, and banks embarked on a program to establish loan loss provisions for their debt.

By 1989, the U.S. Government also became certain that the debtor nations could not repay their loans. Hence, Secretary of Treasury Nicholas Brady proposed a plan that set up permanent reductions in loan principal and existing debt-servicing obligations. The objective of the creation of Brady Bonds was to lower debt in these countries by converting distressed sovereign debt into a number of different types of bonds (Anderson, 2000). Furthermore, banks could exchange claims on these debts for tradable assets, which enabled them to get the debt off their balance sheets. Between 1989 and 1994, private lenders forgave US$ 61 billion in loans, which formed about one third of the total outstanding debt (FDIC, 1997). In return, the eighteen countries that endorsed the Brady plan agreed to domestic economic reforms that would allow them to service their remaining debt.

To conclude this section, despite the many warning signals that Latin America's debt level was unsustainable and that U.S. banks were overexposed to that debt, market participants did not acknowledge the problem until it had already exploded. The outcome was a crisis that entailed a decade of negotiations and multiple attempts at debt rescheduling to resolve the problems at substantial cost to the citizens of Latin America and other developing countries.

Some lessons can be drawn from the debt crises of the 1980s. One, only fiscal reform cannot solve a debt crisis. Austerity must be a component of a broader strategy, and not the strategy itself. Two, the Latin American experience accentuates the significance of economic growth in a recovery. A country that is able to grow is able to repay its debts. Third, Latin America's Brady Bond program recommends a model for a market-friendly default that can lower debt overhang without exiling a country from international capital markets.

5.4 Russia's Financial Crisis of 1998

In the mid-1990s, Russia was emerging out of post-Soviet period to a market economy. There was vast social dislocation, decrease in living standards, and inflation remained in excess of 300 percent. Many Russians did not possess savings for basic needs. Barter prevailed in many parts of the economy and the concept of debt repayment or legal enforcement was yet to be recognized. High inflation was ascribed to a lack of fiscal discipline as the government ran enormous budget deficits financed by the Central Bank of Russia. Rampant tax evasion and capital flight prevailed.

In 1995, there were some weak efforts to slash the budget deficits. The government attempted to control the money growth by maintaining the exchange rate of the ruble *vis-à-vis* the U.S. dollar within a preannounced band.

Inflation was reduced to less than 50 percent by 1996 and to under 15 percent by the onset of the East Asian financial crisis. Russia was able to access credit from the international capital markets and foreigners acquired government issued paper. The strong current account, soaring international reserves and an appreciation in exchange rate shielded up the challenges of high debt servicing costs.

The situation in the pre-crisis year 1997 did not exhibit obvious warnings of financial turmoil. 1997 was the first year since the end of the 1980s when GDP growth had been positive with an annual rate of 0.8 percent. The rate of inflation stood at 11 percent, very low when compared with the three-digit rates that were prevalent in the first half of the 1990s. The real interest rate fell to lower levels, and banks started to expand credits to the real sector. The sovereign ratings of Russia were satisfactory. By the beginning of the East Asian financial crisis there had been a stabilization of domestic debt. Russia successfully restructured its external debt and entered the Eurobond market.

The low oil prices coupled with the onset of the East Asian financial crisis in 1997 led to a sudden worsening in Russia's terms of trade. There was a 25 percent drop in the total exports and there were lower inflows from international capital markets coupled with increasing cost of access to international capital (Srinivas, 2018).

With a worsening balance of payments situation during 1997-98, Russia faced international debt repayments of US$ 20 billion. The Bank of Russia mediated in the market, selling foreign exchange reserves to safeguard the exchange rate.

Market sentiment had weakened quickly and despite borrowings from the international financial institutions, there was a swift decline in the reserves position. In August 1998, the domestic financial system collapsed, the ruble crashed, the state defaulted on its internal debt, and the anti-inflationary monetary policy was given up. Russia witnessed one of the most destructive crises in its history. Though there was a stabilization of the volume of government debt in real terms, rollover risks had been growing at the time of the beginning of the East Asian crisis. A number of factors such as the chronic fiscal crisis, the costs of macroeconomic stabilization, and mistakes in monetary policy were attributed to the Russian financial meltdown but it was the lack of debt management by the state that made the domestic financial system particularly vulnerable to external shocks.

There was no coherence between institutions as the Duma refused to accept the principal elements of the fiscal program prescribed by the IMF. The inability of the Russian Government to implement a coherent set of economic reforms led to a severe erosion in investor confidence and a chain reaction that can be likened to a run on the central bank. Investors fled the market by selling rubles and Russian assets such as securities, which also put downward pressure on the ruble. This forced the Central Bank of the Russian Federation to spend its foreign reserves to defend its currency, which in turn further eroded investor confidence and undermined the ruble. As a result, there was no credible macroeconomic policy response in the first six months of the crisis. By February 1999, the ruble had lost 70 percent of its value against the dollar and inflation was about 90 percent. The country announced across the board suspension of debt-service payments including ruble denominated debt and suspension of private sector external payments.

Because of the unmanageable external debt and threat of an uncontrollable hyper-inflation instilled, fiscal discipline was introduced in the Russian budget of 1999.

Russia came back from the financial crash rather quickly. One reason for this recovery was the rapid increase in world oil prices during 1999-2000 with Russia running a massive trade surplus in 1999 and 2000. Another cause was that domestic industries, such as food processing, had benefited from the devaluation, which caused a steep increase in the prices of imported goods. Moreover, since the economy was operating to such a large degree on barter and other non-monetary instruments of exchange, the financial collapse had far less of an impact on many producers than it would had the economy been dependent on the banking system. Finally, the economy had been supported by an infusion of cash.

Some lessons can be drawn. First of all, while a favorable combination of factors can mislead governments into thinking that monetary and fiscal policy can be loosened with little adverse impact, practice shows that any long-term imbalance seems to lead to a severe shock sooner or later (Aleksashenko, 2010). In 1998, a history of macroeconomic imbalances led to an overload of short-term debt in Russia. Secondly, the Russian experience demonstrated that when battling a crisis, policymakers must identify all of its origins and address each one of them, never assuming that anyone will resolve itself. Investors understand the problems just as well as policymakers do, and so are prepared to provide policymakers some time—but they are not ready to believe in wonders. Secondly, attention should be accorded to the vulnerability of the exchange rate regime to changes in commodity prices (Gaidar, 1999). Lastly, the size of the rescue package counts. IMF assistance to Russia was unable to pacify the markets and give policymakers adequate time to reinstate budget discipline. Consequently, Russia was only able to tackle its problems by rescheduling its debt and breaking out of the exchange rate band.[2]

5.5 Turkey's Financial Crisis of 2001

In cooperation with the IMF, Turkey designed a stabilization program in 1998 to lower inflation and entered into an IMF Stand-By Arrangement (SBA) in December 1999. Its main pillars included an exchange rate anchor, that is, a crawling peg with a preannounced exit strategy that would alleviate the usual risks of real appreciation for exchange-rate based stabilizations, "currency-board rules" which excluded the possibility of sterilized foreign exchange intervention, fiscal consolidation through a large upfront adjustment in the primary fiscal deficit and a comprehensive agenda of structural reforms (Macovei, 2009). The program also incorporated an ambitious privatization scheme.

To facilitate foreign ownership, a constitutional amendment was approved permitting international arbitration for contracts between the state and foreign investors. The government also promised to keep capital flows free from any control and to desist from intensifying trade restrictions (IMF, 1999). The government declared it would cut spending *via* a reduction in labor costs and a reform of social programs; wages of public sector employees were to be frozen in real terms, while the financing and accessibility of crucial social programs, including social security, would be cut (IMF, 1999a).

Though the program seemed quite fruitful initially, this did not last long. Inflation began to go down, though more slowly than expected. Interest rates, on the other hand, dropped much more than anticipated. This, coupled with the steady real exchange rate appreciation, stimulated a boom in domestic demand and resulted in an expansion of the current account deficit. Meanwhile, fiscal consolidation and structural reforms lingered behind, fuelling market worries with regard to the SBA program.

It was in October 2000 that Demirbank, a key primary dealer and investor in government securities very much dependent on overnight funds, announced that it could no longer refinance itself on the market. Restricted by its ceilings on net domestic assets, the central bank declined to lend to Demirbank, compelling it to sell part of its government securities portfolio and prompting a significant increase in secondary market interest rates and further sale waves on the secondary market. Confronted with an adverse impact on other problematic banks and the Treasury's borrowing capacity, the central bank ultimately infused liquidity in the system in November 2000. This supported in preventing interest rates from rising steeply but raised the drain on official reserves. The IMF promised to support the program and replenished the stock of official reserves, hence soothing the markets. This did not happen for long since the lira continued to be overvalued due to the sluggish decline in inflation. Nervous investors withdrew US$ 5 billion out of Turkey on 19 February alone. The foreign exchange reserves of the central bank, amounting to less than US$ 20 billion, were at a risk of being exhausted. As authorities tried to maintain the managed exchange rate regime, there was a sharp escalation in overnight interest rates which obstructed the government's ability to raise money. At this point, the devaluation of the Turkish lira appeared unavoidable. When the pegged exchange rate system was halted, the lira instantly depreciated about 30 percent against the U.S. dollar (Orhangazi, 2002).[3]

The financial havoc and the breakdown of the peg had dreadful impacts on the real economy. In 2001, real GDP fell by 5.7 percent and investments crumpled in volume terms by 30 percent while industrial output went down by 8.7 percent. Exports of goods and services dropped marginally by about 1 percent compared to 2000, but imports fell by almost 8 percent in volume terms due to depressed domestic demand and sharp depreciation of the currency. Unemployment rate soared to 8.4 percent in 2001 and 10.4 percent in 2002 from 6.5 percent in 2000. Public debt surged following the depreciation of the lira and the recapitalization of banks from 38.2 percent of GDP at the end of 2000 to 74.1 percent of GDP at the end of 2001 (Macovei, 2009). The banking crisis had impacted about one quarter of Turkey's 81 banks, registering a loss to the budget of about 30 percent of GDP.

Right after the crisis, far-reaching reform and policy initiatives were undertaken. In May 2001, the Banking Regulation and Supervision Agency initiated a comprehensive restructuring program for the banking system which comprised of four major pillars: (a) a restructuring of the state banks; (b) a prompt resolution of the banks under Savings Deposit Insurance Fund (SDIF); (c) a strengthening of the private banks; and (d) a strengthening of the regulatory and supervisory framework (Rabobank, 2013).

To reinforce the capital structures of the state banks, a total of US$ 22 billion was given by the SDIF at the end of 2001. State banks were strengthened through mergers and privatized. Banks under SDIF control were liquidated, merged with or handed over to another bank. Moreover, US$ 28 billion in total was transferred to banks under SDIF control to boost their capital structures.

The regulatory and supervisory framework was strengthened by various revisions in banking laws, consistent with international best practices and especially EU directives. To reduce financial risks, capital adequacy ratios for Turkish banks were increased to 12 percent while international regulations demanded just 8 percent (Rabobank, 2013). Lending in foreign currencies was only permitted for companies and individuals with revenues in foreign currency, minimizing the foreign exchange mismatch on bank balance sheets.[4]

With respect to the factors responsible for the crisis, the primary one was the combination of a fragile banking sector along with a high public sector borrowing requirement (Ozatay and Sak, 2002). The public sector borrowing requirements, which comprised both the general government budget as well as the state-owned enterprises and other quasi-fiscal deficits, were quite huge, hovering above 10 percent of GDP during 1999-2002. Further, several banks were taken over by the authorities (six banks in November 1999 and additional two banks in September 2000). Again, the financing of the budget deficits by the banking sector resulted in the accumulation of currency and maturity mismatches on the balance sheets of commercial banks, which could not borrow long-term in domestic currency. On the other hand, state-owned banks had accumulated significant 'duty' losses and were also involved in unhealthy lending practices. Although both the private and the state banks had mishandled risks prior to the crisis, the nature of the problem differed.[5]

There were also other vulnerabilities that existed and prepared the ground for the collapse of the Turkish lira (Ozkan, 2005). One, the external position deteriorated as foreign debt levels surged from about US$ 3 billion in 1971 to over US$ 100 billion or nearly 60 percent of GDP in 2000. This was aggravated by a sharp upsurge in short-term borrowing since 1996, when commercial banks implemented a forceful borrowing strategy at the short end of the maturity scale. Moreover, the inability to reduce inflation below levels compatible with the targeted exchange rate resulted in a loss of external competitiveness. Two, the weak financial and banking sector embraced a risky strategy for financing the rising public sector needs, which led to the liquidity squeeze in November 2000. Thirdly, a major cause behind the crisis can be attributed to the uncontrollably growing domestic debt stock. The worsening of the fundamentals before the onset of the crisis did not disturb the policymakers or the profit-making banking sector too much, under conditions of easy access to capital markets. The dangers of rapid capital account liberalization without any fiscal adjustment had become obvious in earlier stages of Turkey's financial liberalization.

However, there was disagreement as to the role played by the IMF in the crisis—unsurprisingly given that the crisis occurred barely a year after the adoption of the IMF-supported stabilization program in December 1999. Some economists [including Akyuz and Boratav (2003), Dufour and Orhangazi (2008)] condemned serious weaknesses in both the design of the IMF program and in its crisis intervention scheme. They argue that the utilization of the exchange rate as a credible anchor for inflation resulted in currency appreciation, thus attracting 'hot' capital inflows due to arbitrage opportunities, in order to finance growing external deficits emanating mainly from the public sector's financing needs. The subsequent build-up of external financial vulnerability ultimately increased expectations of a currency-depreciation and resulted in capital outflows which led to a rise in interest rates.

In conclusion, Turkey's experience confirms the theories which state that financial liberalization needs to occur in a strong institutional and regulatory environment, characterized by sound bank regulation and supervision, effective law enforcement and good governance in the private and public sectors. The Turkish economy did not possess these features at all.[6]

Certain lessons can be drawn from the experiences of Turkey. One, the health of the banking system is very crucial. Transparent recognition of losses is vital, followed up, if necessary, by adequate fiscal support to restore solvency and confidence. Financial and operational weaknesses in banks need to be addressed promptly. Properly designed reforms minimize economic and financial losses and help restore momentum for economic growth.

Two, while fiscal retrenchment in the midst of a crisis may not be the best option in all cases, if there is a need to restore government solvency, bold measures can help expedite economic recovery by boosting confidence.

Three, central bank independence, along with explicit inflation targets and a coherent fiscal policy, can be very effectual in overcoming entrenched expectations of high inflation.

5.6 Argentina's Financial Crisis of 2001

It was during 2001-02 that Argentina witnessed one of the worst economic crises in its history. GDP plunged by 20 percent over 3 years, inflation reignited, the country defaulted on its sovereign debt, the banking system was paralyzed and the Argentine Peso that was pegged to the US$ reached lows of Arg$ 3.90 to US$ in June 2002.[7]

Argentina was trapped in a monetary policy regime that limited policy choices. Escalating fiscal deficits, government's high off-budget activities and extensive transfers of over 30 percent to provinces from federal budgets and interest repayments constrained the country's policy options to a large extent. The share of exports in the economy was limited. Debt service payments were absorbing three-fourths of the export earnings. With mounting debt and given the currency's free fall, Argentina defaulted on government debt and the currency board collapsed.

Argentina's crisis required an IMF Stand-By Arrangement of US$ 14 billion and an international support package of US$ 40 billion. The macroeconomic stabilization program sought to bring public sector surplus to 1.5 percent of GDP from 0.5 percent of GDP and reduce fiscal deficit from 6.4 percent to 3 percent of GDP. Despite these interventions, GDP growth continued to decline, falling by 11 percent in 2002 with unemployment surging above 20 percent. The country passed a zero deficit law and made radical policy changes as it ran out of funding options.

The Argentine crisis emanated from a combination of weakness in balance sheets and the inability to frame an efficient policy response (Geithner, 2013). The fragility that turned out to be serious was in the public sector debt dynamics, which were made explosive by the impacts of a prolonged economic slump and the limitations in rolling over debt. The inability to provide a policy response arose from a combination of economic constraints and political factors, primarily meagre political support and resolve.

Though the interaction between fiscal policy and the currency board arrangement played important roles in Argentina's transformation into a crisis country, there were also other factors, including unfavorable external developments. The currency board, though it initially played a vital role in attaining disinflation, was an inherently risky enterprise as it transformed over time from being a confidence-enhancing to becoming a confidence-damaging factor. After inflation had stabilized at low levels, the justification for maintaining a fixed exchange rate was weak because of the economy's structural characteristics. Again, by lending credibility to the exchange rate peg, the currency board arrangement permitted Argentina's public sector to continue borrowing excessively in the international capital markets, thereby increasing the risk of the eventual collapse. Finally, when the economy slipped into recession, the board became a liability in the context of a buildup of sizeable foreign-currency denominated public debt.

Other responsible factors for the downturn included a cyclical correction following rapid growth in 1996 and 1997, a downward adjustment in purchases of durables, an increase in political uncertainty, and declining consumer confidence (Geithner, 2013). Still, another cause for the slowdown was linked with the impact of the Russian default on emerging market bond prices which affected not only private investment in Argentina, through higher financing costs, but also consumption.

The gravity of the crisis—and the fact that it struck a country whose economy had performed quite satisfactorily in a succession of IMF-supported programs—make it especially useful to draw the lessons of the crisis for other countries and for the IMF. The Argentine case holds lessons for crisis prevention, crisis management, and for the design of IMF-supported programs.

Argentina's experiences serve as an example of the complex dynamic interactions among various sources of vulnerability that crises frequently involve, and, in view of these interactions, of how difficult it is to resolve the crisis once the country is struck by it.

The crisis showed that much more attention has to be accorded to sovereign debt and the debt dynamics, both with regard to crisis prevention and resolution. The experience suggested a more cautious review of debt levels. The need for a systematic and disciplined analysis of debt sustainability also inspired IMF work in this area, and has influenced decisions on exceptional access and prolonged use of Fund's resources, in a bid to hit the right balance between supporting a member undergoing difficulties and safeguarding IMF resources.

In terms of crisis resolution, the Argentine crisis exhibited the significance of timely debt restructuring in cases in which the debt dynamics have become irreversible. Once a debt restructuring has become unavoidable, measures to delay it are likely to increase the costs of the crisis and further complicate its resolution.

Important lessons for exchange rate regimes can also be drawn from the crisis. A currency board sets much more stringent demands than other arrangements on fiscal and financial policies, as well as on the flexibility of trade and the labor market. Based on the structure of the Argentine economy, a peg to the U.S. dollar was perhaps not a perfect arrangement once inflation was lowered to single digit.

Another lesson drawn was that it is important to prioritize underlying structural problems over simple macro-level data. Argentina produced very positive 6 percent annual GDP growth from the execution of its 'convertibility plan' through 1997 and had its overall debt levels in check. However, the GDP growth hid the high levels of increased borrowing that could not be tampered in an economic downturn.

Further, one lesson was that a peripheral nation can make sovereign decisions regarding whether to continue to service its debt. If a country selects to break the monopoly of international financial markets and the IMF, it can do so unilaterally as Argentina's experience discloses.

Finally, the crisis illustrated the danger of depending on unstable foreign flows. Argentina did not pay attention to the lessons derived from the oil crises of the 1970s, choosing to support its fiscal deficit with external financing. Obtaining attractive spreads versus U.S. Treasury incentivized this policy but left them exposed when investor sentiment changed in the aftermath of external crises. Portfolio investment should be more carefully scrutinized in comparison to FDI and private bank lending, as its high level of liquidity permits investors to exit the marketplace at the first sign of worry.[8]

5.7 European Debt Crisis

The European debt crisis generally unfolded in 2010 when problems in the euro area were witnessed. The euro currency area had become very large and diverse with the anti-inflation mandate of the European Central Bank (ECB) being too restrictive. There existed no fiscal mechanisms to transfer resources across regions.

Initially, the first phase of the GFC was in August 2007, with the initiation of liquidity operations by the ECB (Acharya and Schnabl, 2010). The global crisis moved into a more acute phase in September 2008 with the collapse of Lehman Brothers. It was the dreadful crisis in late 2008 and early 2009 that distressed Europe as much as the United States.

Through 2008 and 2009, little attention was accorded to European sovereign debt. The focus, instead, was on the steps undertaken by the ECB to address the global financial shock. The ECB slashed short-term interest rates, provided extensive euro-denominated liquidity, and entered into currency swap arrangements to facilitate access by European banks to dollar-denominated liquidity.

But the GFC had asymmetric impacts across the euro area. Cross-border financial flows dried up in late 2008, with investors repatriating funds to home markets and reviewing their international exposure levels (Milesi-Ferretti and Tille, 2011). This process disproportionately affected countries with the maximum dependence on external funding, particularly international short-term debt markets.[9]

Some distinctive features of monetary union were also responsible for the crisis (Copelovitch *et al.*, 2016). These included the following: a single monetary policy for countries with widely differing macroeconomic settings; the lack of fiscal policy coordination among Euro member states; fragmented financial regulation; and the absence of a credible no-bailout commitment.

Nevertheless, despite these unique aspects of EMU, the order of events in the Euro crisis also closely mirrored those of the past crises in Latin America and East Asia, among others. Within the euro zone, massive capital flows from the North to the periphery led to a boom, and then a bubble, in the periphery.

Yet, the euro area sovereign debt markets stayed relatively calm during 2008 and most of 2009. During this period, the major concentration was on stability of the area-wide banking system, with country-specific fiscal risks remaining in the background. Moreover, the relatively low pre-crisis public debt ratios of Ireland and Spain provided some reassurances that these countries could absorb the likely fiscal costs linked to a medium-size banking crisis.

For the euro area, the GFC prompted a major revaluation among investors of the sustainability of rapid credit growth and huge external deficits. Subsequently, this took the form of large outflows of private sector capital, the tightening of credit conditions, and a shuddering halt in construction activity, with national banking systems grappling with the twin problems of increasing estimates of loan losses and a liquidity squeeze in funding markets (Lane, 2012). The total effect of domestic recessions, banking-sector distress, and the drop in risk appetite among international investors created the conditions for a sovereign debt crisis.

In late 2009, the European debt crisis moved into a new phase when some countries posted larger-than-expected increases in deficit/GDP ratios.[10] Moreover, the scale of the recession and increasing estimates of prospective banking-sector losses on bad loans in some countries also had a negative indirect impact on sovereign bond values, since investors realized that a worsening banking sector posed fiscal risks (Mody and Sandri, 2012).

These negative developments were demonstrated in rising spreads on sovereign bonds whereas the annual spread on ten-year sovereign bond yields between Germany and countries such as Greece, Ireland, Portugal, Spain, and Italy was close to zero prior to the crisis. It must be understood that sovereign debts from these countries are all denominated in a common currency, the euro, so that differences in expected yield primarily denote perceived credit risks and differences in volatility.

Greece was the first country to be locked out of the bond market in May 2010, followed by Ireland in November 2010, and Portugal in April 2011. In June 2012, Spain and Cyprus also sought official funding.[11] What follows next is a brief description of the experiences of Greece, Ireland and Portugal with respect to the debt crisis.

The Greek economy was staggering because of massive public debt and loss of market access. High fiscal deficits and reliance on foreign borrowing stimulated demand. Similarly, entry to euro area had assisted Greece to access low cost credit and strengthen domestic demand with an average growth rate of 4 percent. The country also implemented pro-cyclical fiscal policies with tax cuts, raising spending on wages and ran fiscal deficits of 7 percent for the period 2000-08.

Health care and pension costs were exorbitantly high at 4.5 percent and 12.5 percent of GDP respectively. Moreover, the business environment was poor with high inflation well above the euro zone average coupled with low productivity. Similarly, the governance system was weak, hardly any FDI was coming in, and the public sector was very inefficient.

Initially, the authorities made meager attempts to address the vulnerabilities such as reducing the fiscal deficit. Worries about fiscal sustainability deepened with a further weakening of the market sentiment. Foreign funding dried up along with a loss of confidence in the banking system. There were sovereign downgrades by rating agencies and sharp rises in non-performing loans.

Greece was also misreporting its fiscal data for access to foreign borrowing. The fiscal deficit for 2008 was revised from 3.7 percent of GDP to 13.6 percent of GDP. Similarly, the public debt data for 2009 was revised from 99.6 percent of GDP to 115.1 percent of GDP.

What Greece required was a strong and sustained adjustment program to reduce fiscal deficits, to lower its debt ratio and improve its competitiveness. For this, the IMF provided a stand-by arrangement equivalent to 10 billion euros in 2010 and bilateral program assistance was also rendered by Greece's 15 partner euro zone countries, in ratio of their shares in the ECB capital. The objective of the Greek program was to restore confidence and fiscal sustainability to regain market access, restore competitiveness and safeguard financial sector stability.

In aggregate, after eight years of turmoil and severe austerity, Greece finally emerged from its bailout program on 20 August 2018. The EU, ECB and IMF provided Greece with 289 billion euros across three bailout programs in 2010, 2012 and 2015. This level of assistance has so far been the biggest bailout in global financial history (McCarthy, 2018). A timeline of important events in the course of the debt crisis in Greece is depicted in Appendix 5.1.

The unprecedented crisis in the euro area also affected Ireland.[12] Initially, the GFC had repercussions on the Irish banking sector. This was coupled with the bursting of the real market bubble and a severe economic downturn, creating massive bank losses and growing difficulties for banks to obtain wholesale financing. These factors led to a rapidly growing deficit and debt ratios. Though in a strong surplus position from 2003 to 2007, the public finances worsened with the underlying deficit peaking in 2009 at 11.6 percent of GDP (Smyth, 2017). The marked rise in the deficit culminated in an Excessive Deficit Procedure (EDP) being launched in 2009 and entry into a formal EU/IMF assistance program in late 2010.

Due to the deteriorating fiscal position, successive governments embarked on a prolonged period of fiscal consolidation from mid-2008 to 2014. In aggregate, consolidation measures of approximately 30 billion euros or 17 percent of GDP were announced. These adjustments were to a large extent set out in the National Recovery Plan and formed a vital part of the assistance program agreed with the EU/IMF in December 2010. This comprised financial support of 85 billion euros over a three-year period with 67.5 billion euros in external support.[13]

All in all, the Irish economy's too much pre-crisis dependence on a credit-fuelled property price and construction bubble implied that it suffered more financial instability than most countries in the downturn.

Ireland formally exited from the Troika bailout in December 2013.[14] After exiting from the bailout, the economy started to get better, registering a growth of 4.8 percent in 2014. National debt fell to 109 percent of GDP and the budget deficit plummeted to 3.1 percent in the fourth quarter of 2014 (Burke-Kennedy, 2015).

In the context of the crisis in Greece and Ireland and fear of euro area contagion, Portugal also encountered a sudden fall in financing.

When Portugal had joined the euro area, it had the lowest per capita income among the founding member countries. Easy financing with euro accession triggered a spending boom and build-up of debt. The country failed to stick to the fiscal rules of EU's stability and growth pact.

The great recession struck Portugal in 2008; that year the Portuguese economy did not grow and fell almost 3 percent in 2009.[15] Meanwhile, the budget deficit stood at 2.6 percent in 2008 and soared to almost 10 percent in 2009. In 2010, the economy grew by 1.9 percent, but the financial position was very challenging.

A number of factors resulted in different, though interconnected, problems that were conducive to the above situation. The first was the sluggish Portuguese output growth. This was primarily due to the lack of structural reforms, namely in the labor market, low levels of human capital of the Portuguese labor force, and the adverse effect of globalization the Portuguese economy suffered from eastern enlargement of the EU and China's accession to the WTO in 2001 (Andrade and Duarte, 2011). The second problem was attributed to the result of monetary integration associated with poor policies. The reduction in interest rates after years of inflation uncertainty and high nominal interest rates led to a type of Dutch disease. The level of public and private indebtedness moved to very high levels, the saving rate plummeted, and price competitiveness worsened continuously reducing the rate of output growth. The third problem concerned the lack of accountability and transparency of political governance.

Portugal ultimately was not able to repay or refinance its government debt and requested a bailout in April 2011; in 2011 the economy fell 1.3 percent and the government reported a 4.2 percent budget deficit. Meanwhile, government debt-to-GDP ratio sharply soared from 68 percent in 2007 to 111 percent in 2011.

On 7 April 2011, Portugal became the third euro area member state to seek financial assistance from the EU and the IMF. About one year after the EU had approved the first financial aid package to Greece and five months after Ireland had sought financial assistance under the temporary crisis mechanisms that had in the meantime been established by the EU (the European Financial Stability Mechanism, EFSM) and by the euro area (the European Financial Stability Facility, EFSF), Portugal could no longer withstand pressure from the financial markets on the financing conditions of its economy.

To resolve the issue, Portugal required an IMF financing program amounting to 26 billion euros. In 2011, the country received a bailout worth 78 billion euros from Europe and the IMF. Its economy shrank as much as 3.2 percent in 2012. During the crisis, the unemployment rate reached almost 18 percent.

After undertaking a host of economic and fiscal reforms, under the supervision of the IMF and the EU, Portugal refused the last tranche from its creditors in June of 2014 and freed itself from international assistance.

Overall, in each of the three bailouts, joint EU/IMF programs were laid out under which a three-year funding would be provided on condition that the recipient countries implemented fiscal austerity packages and structural reforms to stimulate growth (particularly crucial in Greece and Portugal) and recapitalized and deleveraged overextended banking systems (particularly important in Ireland). As the scale of required funding far exceeded normal IMF lending levels, the EU became the principal source of funding. At that time, it was also agreed upon to establish a temporary EFSF that could issue bonds on the basis of guarantees from the member states in order to provide official funding in any future crises. Moreover, the pre-existing European Stability Mechanism, which had earlier only been utilized for balance-of-payments foreign currency support for non-euro member countries, was adjusted to provide funding also for euro member countries.

The high outstanding sovereign debt levels and the importance of circumventing future fiscal crises in the euro area induced reforms to the fiscal rules in the euro area with the Treaty on Stability, Coordination and Governance in the Economic and Monetary Union, or more plainly the Fiscal Stability Treaty.[16] There was then the Fiscal Compact which implies the fiscal chapter of the Treaty (Title III). It binds 22 member states: the 19 member states of the euro zone, plus Bulgaria, Denmark and Romania.[17]

An important lesson learnt from the debt crisis was that for ensuring the long-term viability of the euro, the policymakers needed to adopt some combination of the policies and institutions—a true euro zone lender of last resort, some type of fiscal policy coordination, increased labor mobility between member states—essential to maintain a monetary union among disparate national economies with large and persistent macroeconomic imbalances (Copelovotich, 2016). In other words, monetary union devoid of fiscal and regulatory coordination was unsustainable.

The second lesson from the European sovereign debt crisis is that borrowing on international markets is a delicate matter. Though there are benefits of such borrowing in some cases, borrowing too much can erode credibility and produce a crisis in the borrowing country.

Another message provided by the crisis is that it was the lack of aggregate demand that exacerbated and elongated the financial crisis in southern Europe. When struck by a sudden stop, there is no choice for domestic fiscal policy but to become more restrictive, and a credit squeeze cannot be circumvented as domestic banks are compelled to deleverage. In order to escape a deep and prolonged recession, active aggregate demand management at the level of the euro zone as a whole is a must. But this did not take place.

In conclusion, the origin and proliferation of the European sovereign debt crisis can be attributed to the faulty original design of the euro. Especially, there was a lack of understanding of the fragility of a monetary union under crisis conditions, especially in the absence of banking union and other European-level buffer tools. Still, despite all the internal political hurdles, the euro area managed to furnish a policy response overcoming many of the institutional weaknesses. However, structural change in the euro area has to be positioned not only at making similar crises much more unlikely to happen but also meant at pulling the euro area's weight behind solving such crises if and when they happen.

Appendix 5.1: Greek Debt Crisis: Chronology of Events

2009	Events
4 Oct.	Newly elected Prime Minister George Papandreou reveals that Greece's budget deficit will exceed 12 percent of GDP, nearly double the original estimates. The figure is later revised upward to 15.4 percent.
2010	
2 May	To avoid default, the IMF and EU agree to provide Greece with 110 billion euros ($146 billion) in loans over three years with Germany providing about 22 billion euros of the EU's 80-billion-euro portion. In exchange, Prime Minister Papandreou commits to austerity measures, including 30 billion euros in spending cuts and tax increases.
10 May	The ECB launches its unprecedented Securities Market Program. The program allows the ECB to purchase government bonds of struggling sovereigns, like Greece, on the secondary market in order to boost market confidence and prevent further sovereign debt contagion throughout the euro zone. Finance ministers also agree on rescue measures worth 750 billion euros, or nearly US$ 1 trillion, for struggling euro zone economies.
2011	
31 Oct.	Prime Minister Papandreou is forced to step down, and economist Lucas Papademos is appointed to head a unity government tasked with implementing further austerity and structural reforms.
2012	
21 Feb.	Finance ministers approve a second EU-IMF bailout for Greece, worth 130 billion euros (US$ 172 billion) including a 53.5 percent debt write-down—or "haircut"—for private Greek bondholders. In exchange, Greece must reduce its debt-to-GDP ratio from 160 percent to 120.5 percent by 2020.

2 Mar.	Twenty-five EU member states—all but the UK and the Czech Republic—sign a Fiscal Compact Treaty mandating stricter budget discipline throughout the union. The agreement includes a balanced budget rule demanding governments to maintain deficits below 0.5 percent of GDP and an undefined 'automatic correction mechanism' for countries that miss the target.
6 Sep.	ECB President Mario Draghi announces an open-ended program to buy the government bonds of struggling euro zone states on the secondary market. The policy shift is aimed at calming volatile markets, and the ECB's strong show of commitment succeeds in bringing down borrowing costs for indebted periphery countries.
27 Nov.	Euro zone finance ministers and the IMF agree to a revised aid deal for Greece, including lower interest rates on Greek bailout loans and a debt-buyback program. The new plan allows Greece to cut its debt-to-GDP ratio to 124 percent by 2020, rather than 120 percent, while committing it to bringing its debt levels 'substantially below' 110 percent by 2022.
2013	
17 July	Greece's Parliament approves unpopular new austerity measures, agreed to as a condition of the ongoing EU-IMF bailout. The approval opens the way for a new tranche of bailout funds worth nearly 7 billion euros.
2014	
10 Apr.	Greece returns to international financial markets with its first issue of Eurobonds in four years. The government raises 3 billion euros in five-year bonds, with an initial yield of under 5 percent—a low rate seen as a mark of a return to economic normalcy. In another sign of renewed investor confidence, the offer raises 1 billion euros more than expected.

2015	
22 Jan.	Faced with deflation and economic stagnation in the euro zone, the ECB announces a 1.1 trillion euro program of quantitative easing to spur inflation and growth. Under ECB rules, however, Greek bonds are not eligible.
25 Jan.	The left-wing, anti-austerity Syriza party wins a resounding victory in snap elections. Incoming Prime Minister Alexis Tsipras says he will push for a renegotiation of bailout terms, debt cancellation, and renewed public sector spending.
30 June	The Greek government misses its 1.6 billion euros payment to the IMF when its bailout expires on June 30, making it the first developed country to effectively default to the Fund. Negotiations between the Syriza leadership and its official creditors fell apart days before, when Prime Minister Tsipras proposed a referendum on the EU proposals.
16 July	Prime Minister Tsipras bends to European creditors and presses parliament to approve new austerity measures, despite a July 5 referendum in which Greeks overwhelmingly rejected these terms. The agreement comes after a weekend of talks in which a Greek euro zone exit was only narrowly averted and opens the way to a possible third bailout program worth up to 86 billion euros. The ECB resumes some support for Greek banks.
14 Aug.	The Greek parliament adopts a suite of economic reforms as part of a new rescue package from the EU, the country's third since 2010. In exchange for the 86 billion euro bailout, which is to be distributed through 2018, EU creditors require Greece to implement tax reforms, cut public spending, privatize state assets, and reform labor laws, among other measures. While the IMF participated in the previous bailouts, the organization refuses to contribute additional funds until the creditors provide Greece 'significant debt relief.'

2017	
Feb.	Tensions over Greece's third bailout grow as the IMF warns that the country's debt is unsustainable. To forestall a crisis that could put the 86-billion-euro program in jeopardy, EU representatives agree to more lenient budget targets, but they refuse to consider any debt relief. Meanwhile, Prime Minister Tsipras agrees to implement deeper tax and pension reforms even as he faces domestic pressure over a weakening economy and rising poverty.
2018	
20 Aug.	Greece receives its final loan from European creditors, completing a bailout program begun in 2015, the country's third since 2010. In total, Greece now owes the EU and IMF roughly 290 billion euros, part of a public debt that climbed to 180 percent of GDP.

Source: Council on Foreign Relations. "Greece's Debt." Available at: https://www.cfr.org/timeline/greeces-debt-crisis-timeline

NOTES

1. In January 1931, Bolivia became the first Latin American state to formally declare a unilateral moratorium on its foreign debts. It was followed in May by Peru, and by Chile in July. In October, the largest Latin American debtor, Brazil, announced a partial suspension of payments of its debts.
2. Though the foregoing paragraphs critically examined Russia's financial crisis of 1998 and the lessons derived from it, it was again in December 2014 that Russia witnessed another significant drop in the ruble's value when a decline in confidence in the Russian economy caused investors to sell off their Russian assets and sparked fears of a financial crisis. The lack of confidence in the Russian economy arose from at least two major factors. The first was the drop in the price of oil in 2014. Crude oil, a major export of Russia, declined in price by nearly 50 percent between its yearly high in June 2014 and 16 December 2014. The second was the result of international economic sanctions imposed on Russia following Russia's annexation of Crimea and the Russian military intervention in

Ukraine (Dorning and Katz, 2014). The 2014-15 crisis impacted the Russian economy and regional financial markets. The Russian stock market, in particular, saw some sharp falls, with a 30 percent drop in the Russia Trading System (RTS) Index from the beginning of December through 16 December 2014 (Kuepper, 2019). By 2016, the Russian economy recovered with 0.3 percent GDP growth and was officially out of the recession. By January 2017, the foreign currency reserves of Russia stood at $391 billion and the inflation rate was 5.0 percent.

3. The lira continued to fall during most of the year, depreciating by about 60 percent against the US$ from February to October (Macovei, 2009).
4. Other regulations consisted of the inclusion of repo transactions on balance sheets. Futures, option contracts and other derivative products were included, under the definition of credit, to limit overall exposure to counterparties.
5. The private banks were more exposed to the exchange rate risk due to a higher and decreasing ratio of foreign currency to lira liabilities, while state banks were more subject to the interest rate risk, owing to their inability to extend financing beyond short-term domestic instruments. Consequently, the prudential indicators of the banking system had worsened to the point where the sector could no longer ensure a smooth financing of the public debt (Macovei, 2009).
6. Moreover, Turkey was also one of the worst hit countries from the GFC in 2008. The country had depended largely on external financing by charging a high interest rate. The external debt and current account deficit had soared, and the lira had become overvalued. In the aftermath of the GFC, the drop in the flow of financial funds, direct private investments as well as exports led to a plunge in the country's GNP. Though it declined to make a stand-by agreement with the IMF, the country was able to recover relatively quickly after gradually lowering the interest rate. Again, there was also a financial crisis in 2018 which was characterized by the Turkish lira plunging in value, high inflation, rising borrowing costs, and correspondingly rising loan defaults. The responsible factors for the crisis included the country's excessive current account deficit and huge amounts of private foreign-currency denominated debt. While the crisis was obvious for a series of major devaluation of the currency, the later stages were exemplified by corporate debt defaults

and by contraction of economic growth. The crisis ended a period of overheating economic growth, fostered primarily by a construction boom driven by foreign borrowing, easy credit, and government spending.

7. A year earlier, Argentina was considered as a paradigm of successful economic reform, inflation was in single digit, GDP growth was quite satisfactory, and the economy had successfully survived the storm of the Tequila crisis.
8. It should be noted that Argentina also faced a crisis in 2018. When the government under President Mauricio Macri, took office in December 2015, it had announced that its economic policies would attract FDI and result in sustained rises in productivity. The currency crisis that struck the country in April 2018 underlined the failure of its policy approach. The government meanwhile secured a US$ 57 billion stand-by loan from the IMF and agreed on a new strategy to resolve the country's macroeconomic imbalances. However, the terms of the loan agreement have kept changing as investors remained jittery. When the IMF approved the new deal with Argentina in June 2018, the government had stated that instead of spending the funds, it would utilize them to raise its liquidity and reestablish market confidence. However, when the peso plunged further, the government and the IMF agreed that Argentina could utilize the loan to satisfy its debt payments and avoid a default in 2019, a presidential election year. The situation continues to be delicate, not least as much of Argentina's public debt is denominated in foreign currencies. The IMF stated that the country's debt "remains sustainable, but not with a high probability" and the real test of Argentina's debt sustainability would begin in 2020 (Guzman, 2019).
9. Inside the euro area, Ireland was the most prominent example: the high reliance of Ireland's banking system on international short-term funding instigated its government at the end of September 2008 to provide an extensive two-year liability guarantee to its banks (Honohan, 2010).
10. As an example, fiscal revenues in Ireland and Spain went down much more quickly than GDP, due to the high sensitivity of tax revenues to declines in construction activity and asset prices (Mody and Sandri, 2012).
11. It should be noted that Poland was the sole EU member to avoid recession during the GFC. Even in 2009, when the whole

EU went into recession, its economy grew at 2.6 percent. This state of affairs can be ascribed to various factors including timely fiscal and monetary stimulus, a large depreciation of the currency, and a relatively big domestic economy, which restricted the nation's exposure to dwindling international trade. Moreover, growth was facilitated by increasing inflows of funds from the EU and a diversified export structure. Another factor that played an instrumental role was its healthy banking sector. Polish banks stayed profitable, liquid, and well-capitalized throughout the crisis. In comparison to most other EU countries, Poland's banks managed to raise lending to the private sector during the crisis, supporting the country's growth (Piatkowski, 2015).

12. Ireland's example is the most extraordinary one among the countries facing debit crisis. In 2007 only, the country was viewed by many as one of the best performers in terms of economic attainments. It had undergone a long period of high economic growth and low unemployment with budget surpluses. The country seemed to be well placed to handle with any economic slowdown as it possessed a gross debt-GDP ratio of 25 percent in 2007 and a sovereign wealth fund worth about 5,000 euros a head. While an extremely low debt-GDP ratio arising from years of fast economic growth may have appeared to provide a significant cushion against any downturn, Ireland's fiscal situation turned out to be too reliant on the strength of its property sector (Whelan, 2011).
13. This included 22.5 billion euros from the IMF, 22.5 billion euros from the European Financial Stability Mechanism (EFSM), 22.5 billion euros from the European Financial Stability Facility (EFSF) and 4.8 billion euros in bilateral loans from the UK, Sweden and Denmark (Smyth, 2017).
14. The term *troika* has been generally used in Greece, Cyprus, Ireland, Portugal and Spain to denote the consortium of the EC, ECB and the IMF that provided a bailout to these member states since 2010 and the financial measures that the institutions have demanded in return.
15. It should be noted that recession had not started only due to the impact of the crash in 2010, but rather with a slump that had been going on for ten years prior to that. During 2000-09, real GDP per capita had gone up by only 2.9 percent and the unemployment rate had soared from 4.9 percent to

11.3 percent. The country did not encounter a housing price boom nor a substantial expansion of its construction sector before the crisis. Instead, the significant expansion in non-tradables and subsequent appreciation of the real exchange rate that followed the large capital inflows from the rest of Europe occurred in the wholesale and retail sectors and in community services (Reis, 2015).

16. The Fiscal Stability Treaty refers to an intergovernmental treaty introduced as a new stricter version of the Stability and Growth Pact, signed on 2 March 2012 by all member states of the EU, excluding the Czech Republic and the United Kingdom. The Treaty came into force on 1 January 2013 for the 16 states which completed ratification before this date. As of 3 April 2019, it had been ratified and entered into force for all 25 signatories plus Croatia, which acceded to the EU in July 2013, and the Czech Republic.
17. The Fiscal Compact demands the new fiscal principles to be embedded in each country's national legislation. The Treaty is aimed at preventing a recurrence of the Greek debt crisis and defending against the potential collapse of the euro currency. Member states need to keep their budget deficit below 3 percent of GDP and ensure their public debt does not exceed or is sufficiently declining towards 60 percent of GDP.

Chapter 6

Summary and Conclusions

6.1 Summary

This section summarizes the different financial crises and lessons drawn from them.

6.1.1 Financial Crisis in Mexico

In 1994, an abrupt devaluation of the Mexican peso triggered the Mexican financial crisis. This crisis was prompted by a reversal in economic policy in Mexico, in which the new President, Ernesto Zedillo, dismantled the tight currency controls his predecessor had put in place.

The U.S. Government had to intervene during the course of the crisis with a US$ 50 billion bailout in the form of loan guarantees. Yields on Mexican debt escalated, and capital markets activity came to a standstill not only in Mexico but across the whole region.

Ultimately, the Mexican peso stabilized, and the country's economy reverted back to growth. In three years, the country was able to pay back all of its U.S. Treasury loans.

Important lessons can be derived from the Mexican experience of the crisis. First of all, with respect to macro-economic policy, there is a need to avoid unsustainable current account deficits. For countries growing at 5 percent per annum or less, the current account deficit should not be greater than 3-4 percent of GDP (Griffith Jones, 1997). Secondly, too much over-valuation of the currency should be avoided as it supports in reducing inflation quicker. However, if there is a crisis, not only will output fall, but inflation itself will accelerate significantly, as it did in Mexico in 1995. The third lesson learnt was that the structure of government debt should be changed towards more long-term paper, even if this denotes higher costs in interest payments. In other words, large scale purchases by foreigners of short-term government debt should be avoided. Fourthly, in very open economies, large holdings of foreign exchange reserves are a must owing to sharp fluctuations in capital flows. Fifthly, capital account should be gradually liberalized and should be undertaken after the economy is properly stabilized. In this context, some steps to deter speculative capital need to be implemented even if they mean some efficiency losses in the short term. Similarly, the liberalization of the financial system should also be undertaken slowly, particularly if it coincides with a period of liberalizing the capital account and of surges of capital flows. Finally, it is also crucial to properly consider exchange rate risks, and of the fact that exchange rate risk becomes credit risk in the case of a large devaluation and may result in sharp escalations in bad loans.

6.1.2 Financial Crisis in East Asia

The East Asian financial crisis originated in Thailand in July 1997 when its currency collapsed, and the country had to give up its fixed exchange rate system against the U.S. dollar owing to a lack of foreign currency resources. This crisis quickly spread to the rest of East Asia and its trading partners, especially Indonesia, Malaysia, Singapore, Hong Kong, and Republic of Korea. There was an outbreak of panic across Asian financial markets that resulted in the widespread reversal of billions of dollars of foreign investment. As the panic unfolded in the markets and investors grew wary of possible bankruptcies of East Asian governments, fears of a worldwide financial meltdown began to spread. It took many years for things to return to normal. The IMF had to intervene with a bailout package for the most crisis-affected economies to help them avoid a default.

The crisis revealed structural shortcomings and policy distortions in the crisis-stricken countries, together with feebly planned financial liberalization and premature capital account opening. A rapid escalation in external capital inflows resulted in excessive credit and asset price growth across the crisis-affected countries. The economies of these countries were also characterized by huge trade deficits, inflated property and stock market values, poor prudential regulation and lack of supervision.

An array of economic and financial policy reforms in the aftermath of the crisis laid the foundations for periods of sustained high growth. Most crisis-afflicted countries reduced their reliance on external financing and strengthened their overall financial stability, with sound macroeconomic fundamentals and policies, flexible exchange rates, and adequate foreign exchange reserves. Still, the region's growth and financial stability were again mildly affected for some time by the GFC.

A number of lessons were derived from the East Asian crisis. One was the maintenance of sound macroeconomic fundamentals for economic and financial resilience. Second was the need to deepen and broaden the financial systems for strengthening financial efficiency and resiliency. Three, regional cooperation to develop effective resolution tools for distressed assets of cross-border financial institutions formed a crucial part of broader financial safety net arrangements (Park *et al.*, 2017). Four, better information is a must for situations to be monitored and actions taken timely. Five, appropriate prudential and supervisory procedures should be intact, and banks should be in a position to assess risk. Seven, a country should not have a fixed exchange rate unless its authorities are prepared to do what it takes—in other words, together with pursuing sound macroeconomic policies, it must have a healthy banking system and a strong reserve position that can withstand a defensive rise in interest rates to fend off speculators. Finally, capital account liberalization must be undertaken with caution. The problem in the East Asian countries was not that they liberalized their capital accounts but that the sequencing was incorrect and that liberalization was only partial.

6.1.3 Global Financial Crisis

The GFC which exploded in 2007, deepened and moved into a turbulent phase by 2008, was triggered by the collapse of the housing bubble in the U.S. bringing many major financial institutions and businesses to the brink of collapse, and entailed government bailouts of extraordinary proportions. About a decade was required for matters to return to normal.

Policymakers around the globe faced the daunting task of stabilizing financial conditions while simultaneously nurturing their economies through a period of slower growth. The G20 framework became the coordinating body for handling the global crisis as multilateral efforts were especially crucial. These efforts were undertaken to close gaps in regulatory and supervisory infrastructure.

The policy actions included programs to purchase distressed assets, use of public funds to recapitalize banks and provide comprehensive guarantees, and a coordinated reduction in policy rates by major central banks. Governments also launched major fiscal stimulus programs.

By October 2009, economic growth became positive, as extensive policy intervention supported demand and lowered the uncertainty of systemic risks to the financial system. Although the speed of recovery was sluggish, there was a rebound in commodity prices, pickup in manufacturing and a revival of consumer confidence. As the world economy came to a close in 2009, the overriding policy challenge was to maintain supportive macroeconomic policies till the recovery was on firm footing.

The GFC revealed a number of shortcomings in national financial architectures, especially relating to (a) the treatment of systemic banks and other financial institutions; (b) the appraisals of risks and vulnerabilities; and (c) the resolution frameworks for financial institutions. It illustrated that financially integrated markets have benefits, but also risks, with great economic consequences. It also underscored the significance of the interconnections among the banking system, capital markets, and payment and settlement systems. It showed that according priority to only one part of the financial system can obscure vulnerabilities that may prove very important.

A lesson drawn from the GFC was that a country will be better off in the face of a global crisis if its own vulnerability is restricted, for instance, if its fiscal affairs are generally stable, if its inflation rate is low, and its internal and external debt position is sustainable. Likewise, a country will be better off if it has enough space to maneuver to respond to external shocks by resorting to domestic policy instruments, primarily fiscal and monetary policies.

There are a number of other lessons that can be derived from GFC. These include, among others (a) developing a global early warning system to identify asset bubbles and excesses in domestic and/or international markets and the systemic risk implications; (b) ensuring that prudential regimes foster incentives that support systemic stability and dissuade regulatory arbitrage, and assure effective enforcement of regulation; (c) establishing special insolvency regimes to be utilized for large cross-border financial firms; (d) boosting the central banks' capacity to provide liquidity and counter systemic shocks; (e) according special attention to derivatives with respect to regulation, disclosure and risk management; (f) widening the regulatory, supervisory, and information perimeter to ensure that all financial activities that create systemic risks are fully captured; (g) pushing the boundary of regulation and supervision to encompass almost all of the financial sector including the credit rating agencies; (h) improving the accessibility and timeliness of existing data, developing new sources, and promoting transparency and disclosure; and (i) increasing cooperation among international agencies to bring together the different macro-financial information and expertise, and identify key risks and vulnerabilities.

6.1.4 Selected Financial Crises

(a) Stock Market Crash of 1929 and the Great Depression: The stock-market crash began on 24 October "Black Thursday" and continued through 29 October "Black Tuesday", when share prices on the New York Stock Exchange collapsed. However,

the days leading up to the 29th had also witnessed massive stock-market upheaval, with panic selling and very high levels of trading interspersed with short periods of recovery.

The crash resulted in higher trade tariffs as countries attempted to bolster their economies, and higher interest rates in the U.S. after a worldwide run on U.S. gold deposits. Unemployment in the U.S. surged from 1.5 million in 1929 to 12.8 million—or almost 25 percent of the workforce—by 1933, a pattern replicated around the world.

A number of lessons can be drawn from the Crash of 1929. First of all, the fact that stocks can lose 40 percent of their value in one month and 90 percent in a period of three years indicates the significance of diversification. Secondly, a number of seemingly undramatic events may produce a setting for a wide price decline. Thirdly, even a market that is not disproportionately high can crash. Both market psychology and the underlying economics are pertinent.

The crash helped signal the beginning of the Great Depression which was the deepest and longest-lasting economic downturn in the history of the industrialized world. In the U.S., it began soon after the crash. Over the next several years, consumer spending and investment fell, leading to sharp drops in industrial output and rising levels of unemployment as failing companies laid off workers. By 1933, when the Great Depression reached its nadir, some 13 to 15 million Americans were unemployed and about half of the country's banks had failed. Though the reform measures implemented by President Franklin D. Roosevelt helped minimize the worst impacts of the Great Depression in the 1930s, the economy would not fully turn around until after 1939.

A principal lesson drawn from the recovery phase of the 1930s was the significance of regime change for avoiding the liquidity trap. Withdrawal from the gold standard by the U.S. in 1933, along with New Deal policies, changed inflationary expectations and led to a sharp fall in real interest rates. The exit from the gold-standard rule reinstated independence of monetary policy which was important for a number of countries with no policy coordination and beset by wage stickiness.

Another major lesson from the Great Depression was that the financial sector should never be left to its devices. Weakly regulated banks helped activate the crash by lending to speculators. The subsequent collapse of many poorly run financial institutions deepened the crisis.

(b) International Debt Crisis: The origin of the international debt crisis did not take place in Latin America, but rather in the sudden shift in interest rates in the U.S. President of the Federal Reserve, Paul Volcker, decided in late 1979 to cut inflation drastically by raising interest rates exorbitantly. The outcome was a massive rise in short-term interest rates in 1980 and 1981 which quickly increased the debt service of Latin American foreign debts upwards and made a debt crisis almost unavoidable. The main offenders, Mexico, Brazil and Argentina, borrowed money for development and infrastructure programs.

When Mexico announced on 20 August 1982 that it could not repay the loan that was due, this commenced the beginning of a decade long international debt crisis. The crisis spread rapidly as the Mexican default was duplicated by other heavily indebted Latin American countries and led to the weakening of international financial market. The Federal Reserve and some international institutions responded to the crisis with a host of measures that ultimately helped alleviate the situation.

As poor debt management was a major cause of the crisis, it was learnt that beyond good macroeconomic policies, effective external debt management encompasses understanding the debt, deciding how much to borrow, and choosing the most suitable available financing. In most countries experiencing debt-servicing difficulties, these conditions for effective debt management were not satisfied. Especially, country after country did not maintain adequate records to determine the extent of their borrowing.

(c) Russia's Financial Crisis of 1998: On 17 August 1998, Russia defaulted on its domestic public debt, announced a moratorium on the private banks' foreign liabilities which was comparable to an outright default, and ended its exchange

rate regime. The intensity of the Russian meltdown surprised the global markets, and triggered a period of severe financial instability.

The Russian crisis was triggered due to unsustainable public debt dynamics, lower productivity and an overvalued real exchange rate, and was not thus mainly a matter of confidence and liquidity. Following the crisis, Russia experienced a dramatic recovery. The major factors included hard budgets for government and enterprises alike and a shift in the macro policy stance toward the two goals of maintaining a competitive real exchange rate and attaining public debt sustainability. Enabling this shift was the decision to devalue and pursue debt restructuring in August 1998.

The lessons from Russia is applicable to any country simultaneously confronting unsustainable public debt dynamics and low international liquidity, and either a fixed exchange rate or a flexible one with an inflation target.

The financial crisis provided an important lesson for the Russian policymakers as it happened at the turning point of economic development, when the market reforms and the macroeconomic stabilization had begun to render positive outcome and the economy had begun to improve after six years of decline. The basic origins of the crisis can be pinpointed to the country's economic structure, institutional environment and political processes. The crisis brought out the interaction of weaknesses in external and internal economic policy which created the difficulties endured by the public at large in the course of the government's attempts to transform a centrally planned economy into a market economy.

Other lessons can also be drawn from the experiences of Russia. The Russian experience also taught that when combating a crisis, policymakers need to pinpoint all of its origins and address each one of them clearly. Likewise, it was learnt that hardening the budget constraint is crucial not only for raising budget revenues but also for permitting market mechanisms to function properly and thus for raising the efficiency of the economy.

(d) Turkey's Financial Crisis of 2001: The financial crisis of 2001 proved destructive for Turkey soon after the pegged exchange rate system was abandoned in the same year. The crisis emanated from a number of factors including inadequate implementation of regulations, insufficient depth of the capital markets, paucity of assessment of risk, too much lending to incorporated institutions by national banks, restricted interest rates, limited foreign asset holding, lack of competition, limits to foreign entry & high liquidity, chronic inflation and a deficit in balance of payments. After the crisis struck, the execution of the detailed structural reform measures along with prudent fiscal and monetary policy not only made the Turkish economy more resilient to adverse shocks and less vulnerable to crises, but also improved the prospects for the attainment of sustainable growth.

A number of lessons can be derived from the experiences of Turkey. The first one pertains to the significance of the swift policy response and the close coordination among the central bank and other institutions. In the case of Turkey, the Central Bank worked in very close cooperation with the Treasury and the Banking Regulation and Supervision Agency to avoid the presence of excess liquidity in the market. Two, the transparency of the operations during the crisis management is of vital importance for the market's perception on the potential fiscal risks, especially pertaining to bank recapitalization. This enhances the credibility of the operations from the perspective of the market participants and the public.

(e) Argentina's Financial Crisis of 2001: To a large extent, Argentina's crisis pertained to vulnerabilities that were already present or indeed were building up during the boom years of the 1990s. The major elements of vulnerability included the public debt dynamics, the limitation on monetary policy imposed by the currency board, and weaknesses on the structural side. Argentina was also vulnerable as its capital account was open and there was a massive amount of borrowing in foreign currency from overseas. An enormous external debt made the country vulnerable to default not only when interest rates rose, but also when the currency depreciated sharply, as this swelled the repayment burden in domestic currency.

The Argentine case draws attention to the limits in the ability of an exchange rate arrangement—even when supported by the policymakers and the public—to correct other aspects of economic policy in a way that ensures stability.

The crisis revealed weaknesses in IMF's surveillance to ascertain early on the vulnerabilities that emanated during the boom period, and in bringing about required changes once these vulnerabilities became obvious. The crisis also demonstrated the widespread effects of a default on the financial system and macroeconomic policies. This experience called for a more orderly approach to debt restructuring.

A lesson derived from the crisis is that more focus must be given to underlying structural problems rather than to simple macro-level data. Another lesson is that exchange rate arrangements are no cure for problems in the area of macroeconomic policy. Despite the relatively strong set of rules governing the conduct of Argentina's currency board, the regime collapsed in relatively short order when domestic and foreign investors determined that the Argentine Government's fiscal policies were unsustainable.

(f) EU Debt Crisis: Though the EU debt crisis emanated from a mix of factors, including the GFC, easy credit conditions during the 2002-08 period that supported high-risk lending and borrowing practices, international trade imbalances and fiscal policy choices linked to government revenues and expenses, the debt crisis actually began when the government of Greece, freshly elected in October 2009, disclosed that its predecessor had lied to its euro area neighbors and the public regarding the true state of the country's public finances. The ensuing worsening of Greece's access to capital markets led it to request assistance from fellow euro area countries and the IMF, leading to the May 2010 announcement of a first conditional assistance package of 110 billion euros. The debt crisis rapidly spread to other euro area countries. This took place through various channels, including trade links and cross-border financial exposures. By the end of 2010, Ireland (on 21 November 2010) and, shortly afterwards, Portugal (on 17 May 2011) needed emergency lending, which was provided

by financial assistance packages negotiated by the IMF, the EU and the ECB. By mid-2011, the crisis spread to Spain and Italy.

Measures were undertaken to resolve the predicament. Crisis mechanisms were established by the EU including the EFSM and by the euro area including the EFSF. Governments in the affected countries executed austerity measures and started to put in place structural reform programs. And the ECB embarked on a peripheral sovereign debt purchase program.

The debt crisis revealed, as witnessed during the East Asian financial crisis, that crises can spread quickly among closely integrated economies, either through the trade channel, or the financial channel, or both.

Another important lesson from the European crisis (and also the GFC) is that regulatory authorities must not only accord priority to microprudential regulation and supervision of individual financial firms. Rather, they need to identify and manage systemic risk, that is, the risks imposed by interlinkages and interdependencies in a market, where a triggering event, such as the failure of a big financial firm, could seriously damage financial markets and adversely impact the broader economy.

The EU debt crisis also brings to light the significance of maintaining financial stability. Banking crises have a strong potential for seriously harming the real economy. In order to reflect their probability and, if they occur, their adverse real impact, the provision of sufficient liquidity and an adequate capitalization of the banking sector as well as mechanisms to facilitate the liquidation of insolvent banks are the key.

6.2 Conclusions

The decade of the 1990s was primarily remembered for the severity of the financial crises that, among others, disrupted Mexico in 1994 and East Asia in 1997.

With regard to the Mexican financial crisis, there is the risk that this type of crisis could be repeated in developing economies. Hence, policymakers should have, as an important policy objective, to aim at avoiding such crises, since they are extremely costly to the domestic economy. In this respect, countries need to pursue coherent economic policies. Similarly, despite the fact that several emerging economies have had serious difficulties with capital flows in recent times, it is vital not to limit the mobility of these flows between countries. The adoption of appropriate measures to reduce the risks that capital flows can create is needed. Macroeconomic fundamentals must be sound, along with a strong fiscal position and external equilibrium. This is equally very essential for improving the supervision, regulation, and transparency of financial systems.

Laying the stage for subsequent crises in East Asia and Latin America, Mexico's crisis was typified by a severe rectification of the currency and the current account, along with a collapse of output and economic activity. Analogous outcomes were witnessed in the aftermath of Russia's 1998 devaluation *cum* default, and both Turkey's 2001 and Argentina's 2001 crises.

The East Asian crisis was essentially unpredicted while its severity was taken too lightly by policymakers. The crisis had widespread upshots, especially for some other emerging market economies. It impacted countries such as Russia, Brazil and some other Latin American countries. The crisis highlighted the risks of excessive short-term foreign-currency borrowing, leading to the twin currency and maturity mismatches that prompted it. It underscored the volatility and the fragility of the international financial markets. It also had a vast impact on the way economic policies are monitored by governments in developing countries. More developed domestic financial markets and current account surpluses were considered instrumental in the formulation of development strategies of an emerging economy. The crisis illustrated the need to strengthen the international financial architecture.

Compared to other previous crises, the GFC, which was triggered in 2007, was quite different in its manifestation. Previous crises had ensued in individual emerging economies or regions. This crisis, on the other hand, stemmed in the U.S., an advanced economy, demonstrating the fact that financial innovation and deregulation had been more prevalent. The crisis was extraordinary by the complexity and multiplicity of contagion channels. The financial shocks stretched quickly from one market to another and from one institution to another, and from one country to another.

In the aftermath of the GFC, due to the strengthened capital buffers, more responsible approaches to balance sheets and better liquidity management, the banks generally did not pose a main systemic risk in most of the developed countries, particularly, the U.S. However, this does not imply that every country and every bank is safe. Likewise, as the crisis also underscored the significance of better approaches to prevention such as improved harmonization of strengthened regulation and supervision as well as more timely and comprehensive information-sharing, among others, countries have been able to draw on a wider set of insights in strengthening both their macro- and micro-prudential efforts. The agenda put forward by the international community led to the emergence of new international standards and best practices. Implementation of measures for capital, liquidity, and systemic oversight were generally successful, and vulnerabilities linked to derivatives and wholesale funding have been lowered. A host of new standards were devised to increase the resilience of financial institutions and market infrastructures, to make financial transactions safer and to reduce the scope for key entities to generate systemic risks. Techniques have been developed to make the resolution of unviable institutions more orderly in the future. Overall, more than ten years after the onset of the GFC, some progress has been made.

To conclude, financial crises have prompted an extensive regulatory reform effort to better adopt systemic risk and strengthen the international financial system. However, new risks are still surfacing as the financial system adapts to new regulations. Learning lessons from previous financial crises and improving the prudential policy framework will make countries better equipped to withstand the effects of future financial shocks.

References

Acharya, Viral V. and Philipp Schnabl (2010). "Do Global Banks Spread Global Imbalances? The Case of Asset-Backed Commercial Paper during the Financial Crisis of 2007-09." *IMF Economic Review.* 58(1): 37-73.

Aggarwal, Vinod K. (2000). "Exorcising Asian Debt: Lessons from Latin American Rollovers, Workouts, and Writedowns." In Deepak Dasgupta, Uri Dadush, and Marc Uzan, eds., *Private Capital Flows in the Age of Globalization: The Aftermath of the Asian Crisis.* Northhampton, MA: Edward Elgar Publishing.

Aghevli, Bijan B. (1999). "Asian Crisis: Causes and Remedies." *Finance & Development* 36:2. June. Available at: https://www.imf.org/external/pubs/ft/fandd/1999/06/pdf/aghevli.pdf

Akyuz, Y. and K. Boratav (2003). "The Making of the Turkish Financial Crisis." *World Development.* 31(9).

Aleksashenko, Sergie (2010). "Lessons from Russia's Crisis." Carnegie Moscow Centre. 2 June. Available at: https://carnegie.ru/2010/06/02/lessons-from-russia-s-crisis-pub-40883

Anderson, Spencer (2000). "A History of the Past 40 Years in Financial Crises." *IFR 2000 Issue Supplement.* Available at: http://www.ifre.com/a-history-of-the-past-40-years-in-financial-crises/21102949.

Andrade, Joao Sousa and Adelaide Duarte (2011). "The Fundamentals of the Portuguese Crisis." *Panoeconomicus* 2: 95-218. Available at: https://scindeks-clanci.ceon.rs/data/pdf/1452-595X/2011/1452-595X1102195A.pdf

Asian Development Bank (1999). *Asian Development Outlook 1999*. Hong Kong: Oxford University Press.

Audiguier, Cindy (2012). "The Impact of the Global Financial Crisis on the Least Developed Countries." *Working Paper* 50. Development Policies. September.

Bhattacharya, Debapriya and Shouro Dasgupta (2012). "Global Financial and Economic Crisis: Exploring the Resilience of the Least Developed Countries." *Journal of International Development*. 24: 673-85.

Boorman, Jack (2009). "The Impact of the Financial Crisis on Emerging Market Economies: The Transmission Mechanism, Policy Response and Lessons." Presented at Emerging Markets Forum. Mumbai, India. 23 June.

Brett, David (2017). "The Global Financial Crisis 10 Years On: Six Charts that Tell the Story." Available at: https://www.schroders.com/en/insights/economics/the-global-financial-crisis-10-years-on-six-charts-that-tell-the-story/

Burke-Kennedy, Eoin (2015). "Strong Growth Sees National Debt Fall to 109% of GDP." *The Irish Times*. 20 April. Available at https://www.irishtimes.com/business/economy/strong-growth-sees-national-debt-fall-to-109-of-gdp-1.2182317

Calomris, Charles (2003). "Blueprints for a New Global Financial Architecture." In Leonardo Auernheimer, ed., *International Financial Markets: The Challenge of Globalization*. Chicago: University of Chicago Press.

Calomris, Charles W. (1989). "Deposit Insurance: Lessons from the Record." *Economic Perspectives*. May/June. Federal Reserve Bank of Chicago.

Camdessus, Michel (1995). "Drawing Lessons from the Mexican Crisis: Preventing and Resolving Financial Crises—the Role of the IMF." Address at the 25th Washington Conference of the Council of the Americas on "Staying the Course: Forging a Free Trade Area in the Americas." Washington, D.C., 22 May. Available at: https://www.imf.org/en/News/Articles/2015/09/28/04/53/spmds9508

Carrasco, Enrique R. (1999). "The E-Book on International Finance and Development." *Transnational Law & Contemporary Problems*. 9(1): 116-26.

Claessens, Stijn and M. Ayahan Kose (2013). "Financial Crises: Explanations, Types and Implications." *IMF Working Paper*. WP/13/28.

Claessens, Stijn, Giovanni Dell'Ariccia, Deniz Igan and Luc Laeven (2010). "Lessons and Policy Implications from the Global Financial Crisis." *IMF Working Paper*. WP/10/44.

Claessens, S., S. Djankov and L. Lang (1998). "East Asian Corporates: Growth, Financing, and Risks over the Last Decades." Unpublished Manuscript. Washington, D.C: World Bank.

Claessens, Stijn and Thomas Glaessner (1998). "Internationalization of Financial Services in Asia." *Working Paper*. No. 1911. World Bank.

Copelovitch, Mark, Jeffry Frieden and Stefanie Walter (2016). "Four Lessons from the Eurozone Crisis—and Why the Future of any Euro Remains Uncertain." Available at: http://blogs.lse.ac.uk/europpblog/2016/10/07/four-lessons-from-the-eurozone-crisis/

Council on Foreign Relations. (Date not available). "Greece's Debt." Available at: https://www.cfr.org/timeline/greeces-debt-crisis-timeline

Davies, Justine (2017). "Global Financial Crisis—What Caused It and How the World Responded." 23 June. Available at: https://www.canstar.com.au/home-loans/global-financial-crisis/

Dorning, Mike and Ian Katz (2014). "US Won't Ease Sanctions to Stem Russia's Economic Crisis." *Bloomberg*. 16 December.

Dufour, M. and O. Orhangazi (2007). "The 2000-2001 Financial Crisis in Turkey: A Crisis for Whom?" *MPRA Paper*. No. 7837. March.

Economic and Social Commission for Asia and the Pacific (1998). *Economic and Social Survey for Asia and the Pacific 1998*. New York: United Nations.

Edey, Malcolm (2009). "The Global Financial Crisis and Its Effects." 16 December. Available at: https://doi.org/10.1111/j.1759-3441.2009.00032.x

Farrar, J.H., L. Parsons and P.I. Joubert (2009). "The Development of an Appropriate Regulatory Response to the Global Financial Crisis." *Bond Law Review*. 21:3. Available at: http://epublications.bond.edu.au/blr/vol21/iss3/1

Federal Deposit Insurance Corporation (FDIC) (1997). *History of the Eighties: Lessons for the Future—An Examination of the Banking Crises of the 1980s and Early 1990s.* Vol. 1. Washington, DC: FDIC.

Frankel, Jeffrey A. (1998). "Preventing Banking Crises." In Gerard Caprio, Jr., William C. Hunter, George G. Kaufman, and Danny M. Leipziger, eds., *Preventing Bank Crises: Lessons from Recent Global Bank Failures*. Washington D.C.: World Bank.

Gaidar, Yegor (1999). "Lessons of the Russian Crisis for Transition Economies." *Finance and Development*. 36:2. June. Available at: https://www.imf.org/external/pubs/ft/fandd/1999/06/pdf/gaidar.pdf

George, Samuel (2013). "Surviving a Debt Crisis: Five Lessons for Europe from Latin America." Bertelsmann Foundation. Available at: https://ged-project.de/wp-content/uploads/2013/03/Surviving-a-Debt-Crisis-19Mar2013.pdf

Geithner, Timothy (2003). "Lessons from the Crisis in Argentina." Available at: https://www.imf.org/external/np/pdr/lessons/100803.pdf

Goldstein, Morris and Carmen Reinhart (1998). "Forecasting Financial Crises: Early Warning Signals for Emerging Markets." Washington, D.C.: Institute for International Economics.

Griffith-Jones, Stephany (1997). "Causes and Lessons of the Mexican Peso Crisis." *Working Papers*. No. 132. United Nations University: World Institute for Development Economics Research. May. Available at: https://www.wider.unu.edu/sites/ default/files/WP132.pdf

Griffith-Jones, Stephany and Jose Antonio Ocampo (2009). "The Financial Crisis and Its Impact on Developing Countries."

Working Paper. Number 53. International Policy Centre for Inclusive Growth.

Guzman, Martin (2019). "The Trouble with Argentina's Economy." *Project Syndicate*. April 10. Available at: https://www.project-syndicate.org/commentary/argentina-wrong-economic-policies-by-martin-guzman-2019-04.

Gwartney, James, Richard Stroup, Russell Sobel and David Macpherson (2010). *Economics: Private and Public Choice*. 13th edition. Cengage South-Western.

Haber, Stephen (2005). "Mexico's Experiments with Bank Privatization and Liberalization, 1991-2003." *Journal of Banking and Finance*. 29: 2325-2353.

Honohan, Patrick (2010). "The Irish Banking Crisis: Regulatory and Financial Stability Policy." Report for the Commission of Investigation into the Banking Sector in Ireland. Available at: http://www.bankinginquiry.gov.ie/Preliminary_Reports.aspx

International Monetary Fund (IMF) (1999). "Turkey Letter of Intent." Washington, D.C.: IMF. 29 September.

IMF (1999a). "Turkey Letter of Intent." Washington, D.C.: IMF. 9 December.

IMF (2009). "Lessons of the Financial Crisis for Future Regulation of Financial Institutions and Markets and for Liquidity Management." Monetary and Capital Markets Department. 4 February.

International Trade Centre (ITC) (2010). *ITC Trademap Factsheet: LDC Terms of Trade during Crisis and Recovery*. Geneva: International Trade Centre.

Kaminsky, G. and C. Reinhart (1999). "The Twin Crises: The Causes of Banking and Balance-of-Payments Problems." *American Economic Review*. 89: 473-500.

Karshenas, Massoud (2009). "The Impact of the Global Financial and Economic Crisis on the Least Developed Countries," Report prepared for the United Nations Office of the High Representative for the Least Developed Countries, Landlocked Developing Countries and Small Island Developing States (UN-OHRLLS).

Krongkaew, Medhi (1999). "Capital Flows and Economic Crisis in Thailand." *The Developing Economies*. 37(4): 395-41.

Krueger, Anne and Aaron Tornell (1999). "The Role of Bank Restructuring in Recovering from Crises: Mexico 1995-1998." *NBER Working Paper Series*. Working Paper 7042. Available at: http://www.nber.org/papers/w7042

Kuepper, Justin (25 June 2019). "What Caused the Russian Financial Crisis of 2014 and 2015?" Available at https://www.thebalance.com/what-caused-the-russian-financial-crisis-of-2014-and-2015-1979012

Kuroda, H. (2008). "The Financial Crisis and Asia: Short-term Challenges, Long-term Solutions." Speech by the ADB President at the CEO Forum. The Asia Society. 7 November. Available at: www.adb.org/Documents/Speeches/2008/ms2008084.asp.

Laeven, Luc and Fabian Valencia (2013). "Systemic Banking Crises Database." *IMF Economic Review*. 61(2): 225-70.

Lane, Philip R. (2012). "The European Sovereign Debt Crisis." *Journal of Economic Perspectives*. 26(3): 49-68.

Lane, Timothy (1999). "The Asian Financial Crisis: What Have We Learned?" *Finance and Development*. 36: 3. September.

Lee, Eddy (1998). *The Asian Financial Crisis: The Challenge for Social Policy*. Geneva: International Labor Office.

Lin, J.Y. (2008). "The Impact of the Financial Crisis on Developing Countries." Paper presented at the Korea Development Institute. Seoul. 31 October.

Lustig, Nora (1995). "The Mexican Peso Crisis: The Foreseeable and the Surprise." June. Available at: https://www.brookings.edu/wp-content/uploads/2016/06/bdp114.pdf

Macovei, Mihai (2009). "Growth and Economic Crises in Turkey: Leaving Behind a Turbulent Past." *Economic Papers*. 386. European Commission. October. Available at: http://ec.europa.eu/economy_finance/publications/pages/publication16004_en.pdf

Malpass, David. 1995. "The Mexican Peso: 3.5 or Bust." *Wall Street Journal*. 11 January.

Marichal, Carlos (2009). "World Financial Crises: Lessons of the Past." *Finance & Bien Commun.* Available in https://www.cairn.info/revue-finance-et-bien-commun-2009-2-page-34.htm?contenu=auteurs.

Marks, Julie (2018). "What Caused the Stock Market Crash of 1929?" Available at: https://www.history.com/news/what-caused-the-stock-market-crash-of-1929

McCarthy, Niall (2018). "Greece Exits Bailout Program But Remains Mired In Debt." Available at: https://www.forbes.com/sites/niallmccarthy/2018/08/20/greece-exits-bailout-program-but-remains-mired-in-debt-infographic/#4ffdbf4670bc

Milesi-Ferretti, Gian-Maria and Cédric Tille (2010). "The Great Retrenchment: International Capital Flows During the Global Financial Crisis." Paper prepared for presentation at the 52nd Economic Policy panel. Rome. 22-23 October. Available at http://econ.sciences-po.fr/sites/default/files/file/Draft_EP_Dec_15_final.pdf

Mishkin, Frederic S. (1996). "Understanding Financial Crises: A Developing Country Perspective." In Michael Bruno and Boris Pleskovic, eds., *Annual World Bank Conference on Development Economics*. Washington, D.C.: The World Bank.

Mody, Ashoka and Damiano Sandri (2012). "The Eurozone Crisis: How Banks and Sovereigns Came to be Joined at the Hip." *Economic Policy.* 27(70): 199-230.

Mohapatra, S., D. Ratha and A. Silwal (2011). "Outlook for Remittances Flows 2011-13." *Migration and Development Brief*. No. 16. May. Washington, D.C.: World Bank.

Musacchio, Aldo (2012). "Mexico's Financial Crisis of 1994-1995." *Harvard Business School Working Paper.* No. 12-101. May. Available in: https://nrs.harvard.edu/urn-3:HUL.InstRepos:9056792

Nanto, Dick K. (1998). "The 1997-98 Asian Financial Crisis." CRS Report. Available at: https://fas.org/sgp/crs/row/crs-asia2.htm

Naudé, Wim (2009). "The Financial Crisis of 2008 and the Developing Countries." *WIDER Discussion Paper*. No. 2009/01. January.

OECD (1997). "Economic Survey: Mexico." Available at: https://books.google.com.np/ books?isbn=9264149716

Orhangazi, O. (2002). "Turkey: Bankruptcy of Neoliberal Policies and Possibility of Alternatives." *Review of Radical Political Economics*. 34(3): 335-41.

Ozatay, F. and G. Sak (2002). "The 2000-2001 Financial Crisis in Turkey." Paper presented at the Brookings Trade Forum 2002 on "Currency Crises." Washington, DC.

Ozkan, F.G. (2005). "Recent Financial and Currency Crises in Turkey: Bad Fundamentals or Bad Luck?" *The World Economy*.

Pant, Bhubanesh (2001). *Financial Crises, Recovery and Reforms*. Delhi: Atlantic Publishers and Distributors.

Park, Cyn-Young, Junkyu Lee, James Villafuerte and Peter Rosenkranz (2017). "20 Years after the Asian Financial Crisis: Lessons Learned and Future Challenges." *ADB Briefs*. No. 85. September.

Piatkowski, Marcin (2015). "Four Ways Poland's State Bank Helped to Avoid Recession." June. Available in https://www.brookings.edu/blog/future-development/2015/06/12/four-ways-polands-state-bank-helped-it-avoid-recession/

Rabobank (2013). "The Turkish 2000-01 Banking Crisis." September. Available at: https://economics.rabobank.com/publications/2013/september/the-turkish-2000-01-banking-crisis/

Reinhart, Carmen and Kenneth Rogoff (2013). "Financial and Sovereign Debt Crises: Some Lessons and Those Forgotten." *IMF Working Paper*. WP/13/266.

Reinhart, Carmen and Kenneth Rogoff (2009). *This Time is Different: Eight Centuries of Financial Folly*. New Jersey: Princeton University Press.

Reinhart, Carmen and Kenneth Rogoff (2008). "Is the 2007 US Subprime Crises So Different? An International Historical Comparison." *American Economic Review*. 98(2): 339-44.

Reis, Ricardo (2015). "Looking for a Success in the Euro Crisis Adjustment Programs: The Case of Portugal." Available at: https://www.brookings.edu/wp-content/uploads/2015/09/ReisTextFall15BPEA.pdf

Romer, Christina D. (2009). "Lessons from the Great Depression for Economic Recovery in 2009." Paper presented at the Brookings Institution. Washington, D.C. March 9. Available at: https://www.brookings.edu/wp-content/uploads/2012/04/0309_lessons_romer.pdf

Sachs, Jeffrey D. (1988). "International Policy Coordination: The Case of the Developing Country Debt Crisis." In Martin Feldstein, ed., *International Economic Cooperation*. Chicago: University of Chicago Press.

Smyth, Dairmaid (2017). "The Recovery in the Public Finances in Ireland Following the Financial Crisis." *Journal of the Statistical and Social Inquiry Society of Ireland*. May. Available at: http://www.tara.tcd.ie/bitstream/handle/2262/82175/7smyth.pdf? sequence=1&isAllowed=y

Srinivas, V. (2018). "Major Financial Crisis: From Great Depression to Great Recession." *World Economic History*. January. Available at: http://taxboard.rajasthan.gov.in/images/major_financial_crisis_2oth_century.pdf

Strauch, Rolf (2017). "Lessons from the Euro Crisis." BBVA Seminar. Valencia. 23 January. Available at https://www.esm.europa.eu/speeches-and-presentations/lessons-euro-crisis

Tabellini, Guido (2015). "The Main Lessons to be Drawn from the European Financial Crisis." Available at: file///C:/Users/user/Downloads/tabellini(2)20150908153140.pdf

Truman, Edwin M. (2009). "Policy Responses to the Global Financial Crisis." Remarks presented at the Ninth Annual International Seminar on "Policy Challenges for the Financial Sector Emerging from the Crisis: Building a Stronger International Financial System." Board of Governors of the Federal Reserve System. Washington, D.C.: World Bank and IMF. 3 June. Available at: https://piie.com/commentary/speeches-papers/policy-responses-global-financial-crisis

United Nations Conference on Trade and Development (UNCTAD) (2018). *The Least Developed Countries Report 2018*. Geneva and New York: United Nations.

UNCTAD (2012). *World Investment Report 2012: Towards a New Generation of Investment Policies*. Geneva and New York: United Nations.

UNCTAD (2011). *World Investment Report 2011: Non-equity Modes of International Production and Development*. Geneva and New York: United Nations.

UNCTAD (2010). *The Least Developed Countries Report 2010*. Geneva and New York: United Nations.

Vasquez, Ian (2002). "A Retrospective on the Mexican Bailout." *Cato Journal*. 21(3): 545-51.

Whelan, Karl (2011). "Ireland's Sovereign Debt Crisis." *Working Paper Series*. WP11/09. May. Available at: file:///C:/Users/user/AppData/Local/Temp/Irelands_ Sovereign_Debt_Crisis.pdf

Wikipedia. Date Not Given. "Financial Crisis of 2007-2008." Available at: https://en.wikipedia.org/wiki/Financial_crisis_of_2007%E2%80%

World Trade Organization (2009). "The Impact of the Financial Crisis on Least-developed Countries." 2 December. Available at: http://www.wto.org/english/thewto_e/minist_e/min09_e/impact_fin_crisis_e.pdf.

Zahler, Roberto (1996). Comment on "Banking Insolvency: Bad Luck, Bad Policy, or Bad Banking?" by Caprio, Gerard Jr., and Daniela Klingebiel. In Michael Bruno and Boris Pleskovic, eds., *Annual World Bank Conference on Development Economics*. World Bank: Washington, D.C.

"Survey: Mexico." *The Economist*. 28 October 1995.

"The Crash: Timeline of the Panic." *Frontline*. Date not given. Available at: http://www.pbs.org/wgbh/pages/frontline/shows/crash/etc/cron.html

"Timeline: Key Events in Financial Crisis." *USA Today*. 8 September 2013.